PRO
BASKETBALL'S
BIG MEN

Action-packed profiles of
pro basketball's Big Three:
Bill Russell, Wilt Chamberlain
and Kareem Abdul-Jabbar.
In a land of giants,
these super-centers stand
head and shoulders
above the rest of the league.

PRO BASKETBALL'S
BIG MEN

by DAVE KLEIN

illustrated with
photographs

PRO
BASKETBALL
LIBRARY

RANDOM HOUSE   NEW YORK

Manufactured in the United States of America

Library of Congress Cataloging in Publication Data
Klein, Dave. Pro basketball's big men. (Pro basketball library)
    SUMMARY: Brief biographies of three prominent basketball stars renowned for their skill and height.
    1. Russell, William Felton, 1934–   —Juvenile literature. 2. Chamberlain, Wilton Norman, 1936–   —Juvenile literature. 3. Abdul-Jabbar, Kareem, 1947–   —Juvenile literature. 4. Basketball—Biography—Juvenile literature. [1. Russell, William Felton, 1934–   2. Chamberlain, Wilton Norman, 1936–   3. Abdul-Jabbar, Kareem, 1947–   4. Basketball—Biography] I. Title.
GV884.A1K56 1973   796.32′3′0922 [B] [920]
ISBN 0-394-82627-2   73-6743   ISBN 0-394-92627-7 (lib. bdg.)

To Aaron, Moss
and a basketball boyhood

Contents

Introduction

This book is about the best of all centers in the world of pro basketball. So it had to be about Wilt Chamberlain, Bill Russell and Kareem Abdul-Jabbar—big men who showed the rest what a big man could do.

Russell became famous as the defensive star of a Boston Celtic team that dominated the National Basketball Association for more than a decade. He was never known as a point-scorer, but the Celtics had enough shooters. What they really needed was a super rebounder and defensive player. That was Russell, and no one ever played defense any better.

Chamberlain, for most of his career, was best

known as a scorer. Indeed, he was the highest scorer in NBA history. Wilt set one scoring record after another, including a season's average of 50.4 points per game. But late in his career, when he joined the Los Angeles Lakers, he switched from scoring points to stopping them and showed the country that he, too, was a fine defensive player.

The newest entry to the world of big men, Kareem Abdul-Jabbar combined the defensive abilities of Russell with the point-making talents of Chamberlain. It took him just two years to lead the cellar-dwelling Milwaukee Bucks to an NBA championship.

Pro basketball had had many truly outstanding centers—Nate Thurmond, Willis Reed, Bob Lanier, Artis Gilmore, Wes Unseld, Dave Cowens and others. But towering above them all in talent and achievement are the Big Three—Chamberlain, Russell and Abdul-Jabbar.

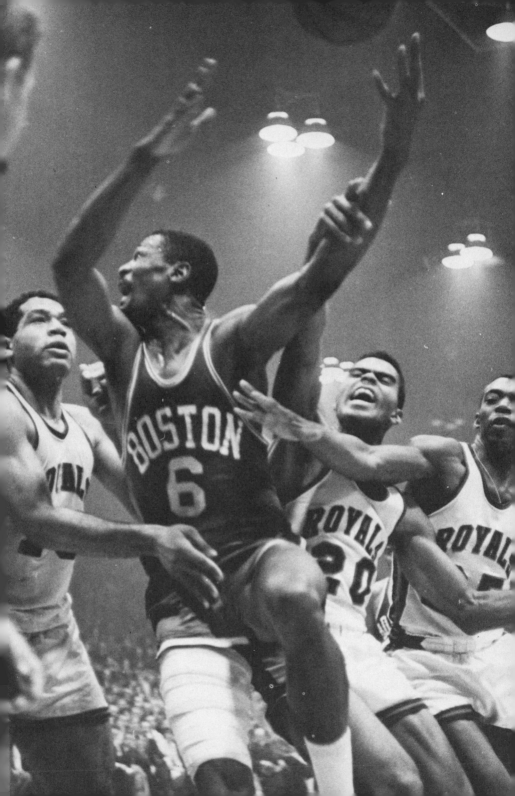

Bill Russell

Until Bill Russell became a professional basketball player, the National Basketball Association had known just one "giant" center—George Mikan of the old Minneapolis Lakers.

Before Mikan, basketball had been a game for smaller men—men with the quick movements and speed to run up and down the court. But when Mikan appeared, after being an All-America player at little DePaul College, he showed that a good big man was more valuable than most good little men. He easily became the NBA's high scorer, and he had no trouble leading the league in rebounds. Because of him, the Lakers won league championships five times in six years.

Mikan showed the coaches a different kind of basketball. Clearly, the winning combination included the talents of smaller guards and forwards and the abilities of the big centers. Basketball had changed, and Mikan was the reason. Soon every team was searching for its own big man.

The Boston Celtics found one. His name was Bill Russell. Three years after Russell entered the NBA, the Philadelphia Warriors came up with Wilt Chamberlain, and for ten years those two dominated the NBA.

Of course there were other good centers during that time, but Russell and Chamberlain were by far the best. They were so good that every other center was compared to them.

"Is he as good as Wilt? Is he as good as Russell?" The answer was always no—until 1969 when the Milwaukee Bucks found their big man—Kareem Abdul-Jabbar.

This time, when the questions were asked, the answer was yes—here was a third man for the list. Other great centers—Willis Reed of the New York Knicks, Nate Thurmond of the Golden State Warriors and Walt Bellamy of the Atlanta Hawks—came close. But there were still only three giants in the magic circle.

Bill Russell was the first.

William F. Russell was born on February 12, 1934, in Monroe, Louisiana. It was the deep South, and in his early years prejudice was as real to Bill as the broiling sun and the fields of cotton.

Bill and his brother, Charlie, might have spent the rest of their lives there if it hadn't been for their father. Mr. Russell had a job in a paper bag factory, for which he earned very little money. One day he became disgusted with all of it—the bad working conditions, the prejudice, the poverty and the South itself. He left the factory and journeyed to other parts of the country seeking a better life for his family.

First he tried Detroit, with its great automobile industry, but he couldn't find a good job there. Then he went to California, which was more to his liking because of the good weather and the more relaxed way of life. When he finally decided to settle in Oakland, he sent for his family.

"Oakland was better, but not much," Bill later recalled. "But to a kid, it was like heaven compared to Louisiana."

The Russell family moved into an eight-room house in north Oakland, which was called "Landlord's Paradise" by the people who lived there. Why? "We lived in an eight-room house, all right," said Bill, "but the eight-room house was really an eight-family house. Each family had one room, and another family lived in the garage. The landlord was able to get nine rentals from this one old building. It was depressing. It was a rotten, filthy place to live, a firetrap."

But there they were, and overall the Russells were better off than they'd been in Monroe. The weather was better, there were better jobs to be had and there was less of the cruel prejudice they had experienced in the deep South. "Oh, it was still there," Bill explained, "but it was a little less obvious."

"I am more bitter about the memories I have

today than I was at the events when they happened," he added. "When I was young I just assumed that was the way it had to be."

Bill's mother and father went to work in a nearby shipping area, one working days and the other nights so that someone would always be home. But Mrs. Russell died when she was only 32, and that caused more changes in the lives of those she left behind.

Mr. Russell had built up a small trucking business with the farmers in the San Joaquin Valley, shipping their produce to the markets in Oakland. It was a good business and, more important, it was his own. For the first time in his life he had no boss. But when Mrs. Russell died he gave it up so he could be closer to home and raise his two sons.

"Dad went to work in a foundry, and he did a good job of bringing us up," Russell recalled. "He was always a man. He raised us by himself, as best as he could, and he taught us to be men, no matter what."

Not only did Bill learn how to be a man, he learned how to be a black man—and proud of it. But he didn't discover his true feelings until he was 16 years old.

"I can clearly remember waking up one morning, and going into the kitchen for breakfast with a pride that has never left me," he said. "I don't know what brought it on, because I had never thought about it much one way or the other, but it changed my life."

Shortly after that day Bill began to learn about other black men. One of his early heroes was a mad tyrant named Henri Cristophe, who for a while was

Celtic John Havlicek (left) chuckles and Bill Russell roars with laughter during a half-time shooting contest.

the Negro emperor of the island republic of Haiti. "It was my first knowledge of a Negro being a leader," he explained. "It impressed me a lot."

Mr. Russell spent as much time with his sons as he could manage, but life for the boys was full of loneliness and frequent separation. "From the day mother died my father never again saw our report cards," said Bill. "I signed Charlie's and he signed mine."

The three Russells moved to an "integrated" housing project near the Coles Elementary School. It was integrated because both blacks and whites called the project their home—but all the blacks lived in one section of the building, the whites in another.

By then Bill was in his middle teens, and he began to show some interest in sports. But interest was just about all he showed. There was little evidence of any talent.

Bill's brother Charlie, who was two years older and a superb athlete, managed to enroll in Oakland Tech, a mostly white high school. There he made a name for himself as an athlete. When Bill entered McClymonds High, which was 95 percent black, one of the coaches was heard to complain: "Why is it if there are two brothers, we always get the bum?"

Bill's entire school life was one of confusion and frustration. "I was always messing things up," he admitted. "It seemed I always got in trouble, and half the time I didn't even know why, or what I had done wrong."

Bill almost failed the eighth grade because of laziness in his studies. He failed to make the homeroom basketball team. He was cut from the football team. He failed in an attempt to become a school cheerleader. He even tried, and failed, to play the clarinet. "I was always off-key," he said.

At that point, the off-key Russell found the first of many men who helped him find some direction in life. After failing to make the high school basketball team as a sophomore (he was 6-foot-2 but weighed only 128 pounds) Bill complained to the school custodian, a man named Art Ison.

"I can't make it," he told Ison. "Those guys are just better than me." Ison looked at the tall, gangly kid who was always tripping over his own feet and said, "If you think so, Russ, then they always will be better than you. They aren't, if you think they're not."

A second man of great importance was George Powles, a white teacher and coach who convinced Bill to try out for the junior varsity team.

"Bill was terrible," Powles later admitted, "but I kept him as the sixteenth man on what was supposed to be a fifteen-man team. He had nothing else, nowhere else to go."

Bill had to share a uniform with a teammate named Roland Campbell because there were only 15. But he had learned to love the game, and he felt important just being a member of the team.

"Mr. Powles saved me, I think, from becoming a juvenile delinquent," Russell said. "He even gave me the two dollars I needed to join the Boys Club. I played basketball there every day, all year, and I worked hard at trying to improve."

By his senior year Russell had gotten himself together, mostly through practice and hard work. Fortunately his awkward body, which had been sprouting like Jack's magic bean stalk, slowed down for a while. He had grown to 6-foot-5, but his weight was up to 160 pounds, and he finally began to show some promise.

But despite his impressive size, Bill was just too

timid on the court. He wouldn't get angry, wouldn't take a challenge from another player. Finally, coach Powles spoke to one of Russell's closest friends, Bobby Woods, and asked for his help. "Get on him," he urged Woods. "Stir him up, make him aggressive."

Woods, a star player who later joined the Harlem Magicians touring professional team, did what he could. It seemed to work, for Russ soon showed a new-found fire and competitive spirit.

And just in time, too, for although he didn't know it, Russell was about to play one of the most important games of his career at McClymonds High. It was against Oakland High, whose center, Truman Bruce, had been named an All-City first-team player.

Sitting in the stands that day was a man named Hal DeJulio, a University of San Francisco scout. He had come to see Bruce, who was being considered for a scholarship.

But it turned out to be Bill's big day. Russell scored 14 points, blocked several shots, pulled down 19 rebounds and outplayed Truman Bruce all game, all over the court. DeJulio was so impressed that he offered the scholarship to Russell instead of to Bruce.

"I was really surprised," said Russell. "Not only didn't I think I was good enough, but I had been living across San Francisco Bay most of my life and I

Russell seems hypnotized by the ball after scoring for the University of San Francisco in 1956.

didn't even know there was a university there. But it
was the only scholarship I was offered, and I took it
because I couldn't have gone to college any other
way."

The boy who had almost failed the eighth grade
was going to college. Basketball was the key to his
education, and Bill was just beginning to understand
that many other doors might be opened in the same
way.

"I took my first trip because of basketball," he
later recalled. "It was the summer before I entered
college, and I went with a group of high school
all-stars through the northwest and into British
Columbia [in Canada] playing other all-star teams. I
began to see how other people lived, outside the
ghetto."

In 1953, Bill entered the University of San
Francisco. It was a small school, so small it didn't
even have its own gym. But Bill loved it there. His
roommate was another basketball player, named
K. C. Jones.

In their first month as roommates, the two athletes
did everything together but talk. Both were ex-
tremely shy, and both had memories of deprived
childhoods that they preferred to forget. But eventually they became close friends.

Bill's scholarship was for room and board, tuition
and books. Spending money was not included, so he
waited on tables and washed dishes in the college
cafeteria for $15 a month. But K. C. Jones had a
campus job that paid him $30 a month, and he was a
generous friend. Whenever he bought something for
himself, like shoes, he made sure he could afford two

pair so that he could give one to Russell.

It was on the basketball court, though, that the boys really got together. With K. C. and a quickly-improving Russell, San Francisco fielded an outstanding freshman team. The fans looked forward to the next year when the boys would be sophomores and eligible for the varsity team, the San Francisco Dons.

In their very first varsity game, however, K. C. suffered a ruptured appendix and was out of action for the entire season. Nevertheless, the Dons finished the season with a 14–7 record, and Russell improved with each game.

By the next season Russell, Jones, Jerry Mullen, Stan Buchanan and Hal Perry were all playing well, and the Dons got off to a great start. In December of 1955 they lost a game to UCLA and then did not lose again for 60 straight games, a winning streak that stood as a national record for nearly 20 years.

Included in the streak were two national championships, in 1955 and 1956. In 1955, San Francisco's victim was a LaSalle College team from Philadelphia led by All-America forward Tom Gola. Russell scored 33 points in that game to lead the Dons to a 77–63 victory.

Bill and K. C.'s last appearance with the Dons was another winning one. They defeated Iowa, 83–71, to win the 1956 NCAA championship. When they graduated, San Francisco's winning streak was 55, and the new team added five more the next season before losing to Illinois, 62–33. It was the first time in more than two years that San Francisco had lost a game.

Most of the credit, of course, belonged to Bill. He was named an All-America center for two years in a row, and his coach, Phil Woolpert, called him "the finest big man I have ever coached or seen in all of college basketball."

In his varsity years Russell dominated the game so much that the NCAA decided to make two rule changes to prevent future Russells from doing the same thing. It became illegal to touch a teammate's shot while the ball was on a downward path, and the free throw lane was widened from six feet to twelve to stop the big man from stationing himself right near the basket and grabbing every rebound.

But what counted in the spring of 1956 was the annual NBA player draft. Everyone knew that Russell would be signed by a professional team—but which one?

Of course every team wanted the college super-star, but the Boston Celtics *needed* him. Head coach Red Auerbach, who was desperate for a big center, was determined not to let this one get away. But that was easier said than done. Because the order of selection for the draft was decided by simply "turning around" the teams' records of the previous season, the worst teams got the first chance to choose their new players. The Celtics had done quite well in 1955–56, so Boston was the seventh team scheduled to pick. Unless something could be done, Russell would be taken long before the Celtics got their turn.

Russell springs up to block a shot by Milt Scheuerman of Iowa during the 1956 NCAA finals.

The Rochester Royals had the first pick. But although they wanted Russell, they were in financial trouble and knew they couldn't afford to sign him. So the Royals decided to pass him up.

But the next team in line was the St. Louis Hawks. They not only had the money, they had the need for a big center, too. But there was one hitch. Before Russell could begin his pro career, he had a date in Melbourne, Australia. Bill and the U.S. amateur basketball team would be participating in the 1956 summer Olympics. Russell would not be free to join the Hawks until December, when he returned from the Games. St. Louis, however, wanted someone who could start right away, so they were willing to consider a deal with Boston.

The Celtics' Red Auerbach offered Ed Macauley, a former All-America center at St. Louis University and Boston's first-round draft pick, to the Hawks for their first-round choice. It was a great deal for St. Louis. With Macauley, a "local hero" and the man they drafted in Boston's place, high-scoring forward Cliff Hagan from the University of Kentucky, the Hawks went on to win five consecutive Western Conference championships.

And Auerbach had Bill Russell, the center he had dreamed of bringing to the Celtics. Red then went to see his future star play in an exhibition game with the U.S. Olympic team. Auerbach was horrified.

Russell didn't just play badly. "He was terrible," said Auerbach. After the game Russell told him, "I don't usually play that bad."

Red grinned weakly. "If you do," he said, "you better stay in Australia, because I won't be in

Boston. I'll be fired, and you'll find me back in Brooklyn coaching a junior high school team."

Russell not only came back from Australia—he brought a gold medal with him. Bill's fine Olympic performance led the U.S. to four straight wins for the world amateur championship.

Russell joined the Celtics in December of 1956, but at first he did not impress anyone. His contract did, however. The Celtics had signed him at a salary of $19,500, which made him the highest-paid rookie in NBA history.

When he became a Celtic, Russell joined a team that had never won a championship. Nevertheless, it was a fine team with several outstanding players on the roster, including Bob Cousy, Bill Sharman and Tom Heinsohn. Boston also had a fine reserve player named Frank Ramsey, an excellent shooter who played both guard and forward. And the center was Arnie Risen.

Risen knew he would eventually lose his job to the big rookie, but he went out of his way to help Russell anyway. "I've never forgotten him for that, and I never will," Bill said. "He showed me what to do, how to play. And every time he did, he knew I was coming closer to taking away his job. I never knew professionals were that unselfish."

Russell learned a lot that first season. "I was the worst shooter in the league," he admitted. "The opposition wasn't impressed by my All-America reputation. There were All-America players by the dozens all over the league. And if I wasn't a very good shooter, it meant I would have to do other things better."

Those "other things," of course, were rebounding and defense. And Russell did them so well he soon became the most talked-about rookie in years.

"He destroys players," Auerbach said. "Take Neil Johnston [who had been one of the league's top scorers for years]. He has a great hook shot, and he led the league in scoring last year. But Bill destroyed him psychologically. He blocked so many hook shots that Johnston started taking them farther and farther away from the basket. It ruined his timing and his confidence."

Auerbach had seen what others only guessed at, that Russell had the ability to become the greatest defensive center the NBA had known. But it would take a while before he could live up to his true potential.

At first Bill had a major problem with the other centers, who tried to rough him up and intimidate him. It worked for a while, despite Auerbach's instructions that Russell fight back. But one day 6-foot-11 Ray Felix of the New York Knicks threw an elbow with really vicious force. Bill turned and swung a punch, knocking Felix unconscious. Russell was fined $25 by the league, but it was worth it. Nobody tried to intimidate him again.

Once Bill made it clear he could not be pushed around by the league's veteran big men, the Celtics became the NBA's top team, and Russell began to make his presence felt. Offensively he was not yet

In his first pro game with Boston, Russell (far left) goes to the basket and is fouled by St. Louis' Bob Pettit (9).

overpowering, but he did finish the season with a 14.7 scoring average. Much more important, however, was his defense and his rebounding. He blocked shot after shot and finished fourth in the NBA for total rebounds, averaging 19.6 per game. He also helped lead the Celtics to their first-ever Eastern Division championship.

Boston then eliminated Syracuse in the first round of the playoffs in three straight games. (In those years the first playoff round was a best three-out-of-five series.)

After beating Syracuse, the Celtics had a chance for the NBA championship, which no Boston team had ever won. The opposition was St. Louis, the team that had given up Russell in the draft. It was a hard-fought, closely-played series, and after six games each team had three wins.

The seventh and final game was a classic. Six times the Celtics seemed to have an untouchable lead. But the Hawks rallied each time and finally went ahead with 1:30 to play in the game. But Bob Cousy led Boston's comeback, and with 13 seconds remaining, he dropped in a pair of free throws to give the Celtics a 103–101 lead.

Then Bob Pettit of the Hawks tied it up with two free throws in the last four seconds, and the game went into its first overtime period.

Again St. Louis stayed alive when, in the closing seconds of the first overtime, Jack Coleman connected on a jump shot to tie the score again, 113–113.

The nail-biting suspense continued in the second

extra period. With 1:28 to play Boston held a slim 122–121 lead. Then Russell blocked a driving lay-up by Med Park, a Hawk substitute. Russell took the loose ball, passed it to Frank Ramsey, who hit a jumper. Boston was ahead, 124–121.

There were 72 seconds to go, and for 70 of them the only scoring was a field goal by Pettit to make it 124–123. With two seconds left Boston's Jim Los-

Russell makes a crash landing after leaping up for a rebound against the Hawks in a 1957 game.

cutoff dropped in a foul shot. But the gallant Hawks
still wouldn't give up. Player-coach Alex Hannum
threw the ball as far as he could to the St. Louis
basket. Pettit leaped up and tried to direct it into the
basket. The ball hit the rim . . . rolled around . . .
and then dropped off. The clock ran out, and the
Celtics were NBA champions for the first time.

In *Sports Illustrated* Russell drew the praise for
Boston's dramatic victory. "He soared over the court
like some gigantic bird," the story read. "Blocking
shots, grabbing rebounds and generally intimidating
St. Louis shooters."

The first season was over. Russell, who had come
in second to his teammate, Heinsohn, in the Rookie
of the Year voting, was a proven professional. He
also began to find his philosophy of life as a
superstar. "I have always tried to be a man, and a
black man proud of his blackness," he said. "I can
honestly say I have never worked to be liked. I have
worked only to be respected."

In his rookie year Bill was the only black on the
team, but his race was never a problem. "There was
a great feeling on the Celtics," he remembered.
"There was no racial trouble at all. We considered
ourselves a proud group of men who had the
distinction of being what no one else in our sport
could be—the champions."

Nevertheless, Russell was not particularly close to
any of the players nor overly friendly with them. "I
had made up my mind I would not become anybody's usual idea of a Negro," he said. "I would not
seek their favor or try to make them like me. I would

just be me, and if that wasn't enough, too bad."

But it was enough. The 6-foot-10 rookie, by doing what he did best, soon earned his teammates' respect. Eventually many of those teammates became lasting friends. His relationship with Cousy, for instance, was typical of what he felt for some of the others.

"We felt something deep and close, but unspoken. I felt, and still feel, that we will be friends for life. We shared locker rooms, airplanes, hotels, cars, taxicabs and a team for six years. But we never seemed able to get beyond exchanging a few passing remarks to each other."

Of Heinsohn, who later became the Celtic coach, Bill said: "He had more ability than any forward who ever played, but he seldom came close to playing as well as he could have." Heinsohn, many felt, allowed a violent temper to hurt his concentration. But he was always recognized as one of the NBA's top forwards.

Russell was a great fan of Auerbach, too. "Given a choice, I would not play for any other man in the world. He cannot tolerate losing, and neither can I."

Fortunately, neither man had to worry much about losing—the Boston Celtics were truly winners. With their first championship in 1957, the Celtics began the most amazing run of championships ever put together by any professional team in any sport. The team would win the NBA championship ten times in the next twelve years, including one streak of eight in a row.

After his first championship Russell took Boston to

Duel of the giants: Russell goes up for a shot as Philadelphia's Wilt Chamberlain tries to block it.

another Eastern Division title in 1957–58. In the first playoff round the Celtics disposed of the Philadelphia Warriors and once again found themselves playing the St. Louis Hawks in the finals.

The teams split the first two games of the series. Then, almost as if to prove his value to the team, Russell sprained his ankle in the third game. Bill was lost for the rest of the series, and without their big center Boston was lost. St. Louis won the championship in six games.

But the following season the Celtics were back on

top in the East. They beat Syracuse in a tough seven-game semifinal series, then regained their championship by humiliating the Los Angeles Lakers in four straight games.

Over the years, Russell became the league's most feared defensive player. But in Bill's fourth year as a pro another big man entered the NBA—Wilt Chamberlain, the towering center of the Philadelphia Warriors. Chamberlain first faced Russell on November 7, 1959, in the Boston Garden.

It was a long-awaited match, and the two super-centers put on a spectacular show. Russell scored 22 points and allowed Wilt *only* 30 (since Wilt had been averaging 45 points, that was no small accomplishment). Bill also picked up 38 rebounds to Wilt's 35.

Boston won that game, 115–106, setting a pattern that held true throughout the years these two giants met. Boston usually won, and Bill usually played the key role by stopping Wilt or at least slowing him down.

Russell's rebounding led the Celtics for a dozen consecutive years, and three times he led the league. But he was never the team's leading scorer. The Celtics had all the guns they needed, with shooters like Cousy, Sharman, Heinsohn and Sam Jones. What they needed was the big man in the middle, the rebounder and the intimidator. Bill Russell was that man, and almost every player and coach credited him with the Celtics' success. "Without Russell," said former All-Star Jack Twyman, "the Celts are just another good team; with him, they're great."

Most of Russell's most dramatic games were against Chamberlain, either during the regular season or in the playoffs. There was a feeling of intense rivalry between the two, and while they are closer today, they were often bitter rivals during their playing days.

"He doesn't have to worry about points," Chamberlain used to say. "It would be nice if I was with a team like Boston, where I didn't have to score, either. Let's see if he can be not only the top rebounder but the top scorer, too."

Russell's answer to such charges, characteristically, was: "How many championship teams has Wilt Chamberlain played for? We do it the best way, the way that wins. You can't argue with a championship."

Russell proved his point in the 1959–60 season when the Celtics won another Eastern championship in a tough series against Wilt's Warriors. Boston then went on to a seven-game victory over St. Louis for the league crown.

With monotonous regularity, the big Boston machine rolled on.

In 1960–61 the Celtics won the Eastern crown in six games against Syracuse and the championship in five games against St. Louis.

The 1961–62 playoffs provided pro basketball fans with one of the most memorable series in the history of the league. After defeating Philadelphia in the semis, the Celtics met the Lakers in the finals. It was Boston with Russell, Cousy, Sam and K.C. Jones, against Los Angeles with its two fantastic scorers, Jerry West and Elgin Baylor.

In the first game, Baylor made a 35-point contribution to the Laker effort, but Boston triumphed, 122–108. Los Angeles won the second game, 129–122, after getting 40 points from West and 36 from Baylor. In the third game, the Lakers were trailing 115–113 with only ten seconds to play when West tied it up with two free throws. Then in the last three seconds of play, he intercepted a pass and drove downcourt for the lay-up, giving Los Angeles

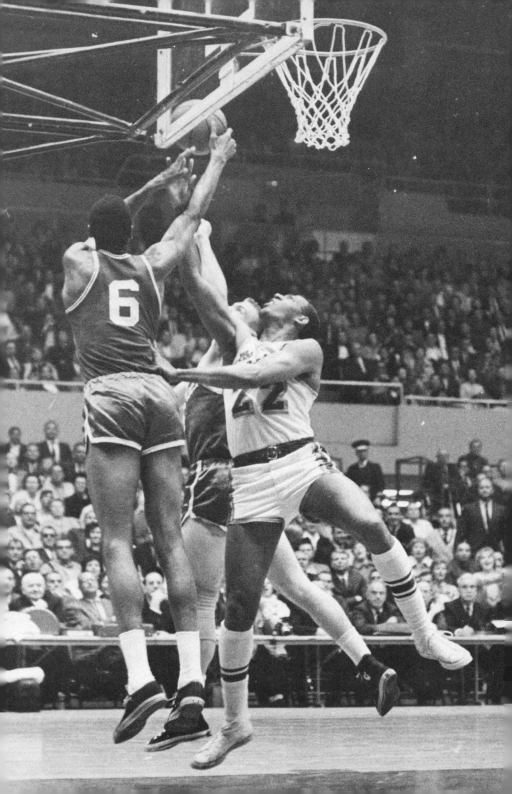

a 117–115 victory. West scored 34 points in that game, and Baylor added another 39.

Boston won the fourth game despite another sensational Baylor and West show. Six Celtics donated double figures to Boston's 115–103 win. The series was tied at two games apiece.

In game number five Baylor scored a playoff record of 61 points, and the Lakers had their third victory, 126–121. But the Celtics evened things up again in the sixth game, wiping out a ten-point half-time deficit to win, 119–105.

The seventh and deciding game was played under the greatest of pressure. With 40 seconds to play in what had been a bruising battle, Los Angeles' Frank Selvy tied the game at 101–101 with a jump shot. The score stayed that way as the clock ran out. The whole series would be decided in an overtime period.

When Los Angeles scored first in the extra period, it seemed as though the Lakers were going to win their first-ever championship. The Celtics' Heinsohn and Tom Sanders had fouled out, and Boston needed some offensive power to stay alive. But then Russell made a rebound shot to tie the score, and before the smoke lifted Sam Jones had scored on a three-point play, Russell had added two free throws and Sam had hit again with a jumper. Boston won the game, 110–107, and another crown.

The following year (1962–63) was a big one for

During the 1963 playoffs Russell (6) and Los Angeles' Elgin Baylor (22) battle for a loose ball under the boards.

Boston and perhaps the biggest for Bob Cousy. The Celtics' high-scoring guard had announced he would retire at the end of the season. But Cousy wanted to leave the game as a champion—and with Russell's help, he did.

The Celtics won their division again, then eliminated the Cincinnati Royals, with Oscar Robertson and Jerry Lucas, in a seven-game semifinal series. Again the Lakers and Celtics met in the finals, but this time it took only six games for Boston to win the crown.

Bob Cousy, who had been one of the legendary stars of the NBA, went into college coaching and finally rejoined the NBA as coach of the Cincinnati Royals (who later became the Kansas City-Omaha Kings).

In his outstanding career with the Celtics, Cousy's passing wizardry set standards of excellence that youngsters all over the world tried to reach. He was a great shooter and a marvelous team leader. Cousy was the first to show fans the behind-the-back dribble, and his fancy ball-handling was as exciting to the crowds as a dunk shot by Chamberlain or a blocked shot by Russell.

In 13 years with the Celtics, Cousy scored more than 18,000 points and made more than 6,900 assists. Ten of those years he was named to the All-Star team.

When he left Boston in 1963 the "experts" said the Celtic dynasty would not be able to survive the loss of their backcourt magician. So it became more important than ever for the Celtics to win again. All the players wanted to prove they were as good without Cousy as they were with him.

With Russell taking on more of the pressure and leadership, the Celtics won their division by winning ten of their final eleven games to finish ahead of Cincinnati. Then they beat Cincinnati in the semi-final round of the playoffs and faced the San Francisco Warriors for the championship. Once more Russell would be facing Wilt, who had moved with the Warriors when the franchise was sold to a group of San Francisco businessmen.

It was oh-so-easy. Boston won in five games, and Russell made sure Chamberlain did not hurt the Celtics at all. It was Boston's sixth straight championship—the first one without Bob Cousy.

In 1964–65, Boston did it again, beating a Los Angeles team that had to play without Baylor, who had been injured. It was no contest, and Boston won in five quick games.

The 1965–66 season started off with a bit of history—financial history. Chamberlain had signed a $100,000 contract with San Francisco, but the Celtic management had offered Russell just $70,000. The Boston center was hurt and angry. "If Wilt is worth $100,000," he fumed, "I am worth more." The Celtics finally saw it his way, and Russ signed an agreement calling for $100,001—just one dollar more than Chamberlain was getting.

That year Boston finally lost the Eastern Division championship, finishing one game behind Philadelphia at the end of the regular season. But the poised Celtics bounced back to eliminate Philadelphia in the semifinals of the playoffs. Then they won another NBA championship by outplaying Los Angeles in seven games.

It was the first time in 14 years that a team finished the season in a runner-up position and then came back to win the playoffs. It took great poise and spirit, but those were the Celtics' trademarks.

A few days after the championship victory, Auerbach announced that he was retiring as coach but would stay on as general manager and vice-president of the Celtics. The man he chose to take his place was Bill Russell. "The only man to coach this team is Russ," he explained. "He is the most respected man in this league, and every player on our team looks up to him already. He does things by setting an

example, and as a player-coach, he is the ideal person."

Russell became the first black man ever to coach an NBA team (in fact, as late as 1973 neither major league baseball nor professional football had ever hired a black manager or head coach).

Bill's first year as player-coach was not a good one. In 1966–67, Boston again finished second to Philadelphia. But this time there was no happy ending. After beating the New York Knicks in the Eastern Division semifinal, Boston was eliminated by Philadelphia in the division final, four games to one. It was the first time since 1956 that the Celtics had failed to reach the league championship finals.

Writers blamed Russell for the Boston slump,

A gleeful mob of fans carry NBA champs Tommy Heinsohn, coach Red Auerbach and Russell around the court after the Celtics clinched the title in 1964.

saying he was not the coach that Auerbach was, hinting that the other players resented him and that they were unhappy at having to play for a black man.

But the "color blind" Auerbach stuck with his coach, and the next year Bill and the Celtics proved he was right. The Celtics looked like their old winning selves in 1967–68, but now the names were different. Cousy, Sharman, K. C. Jones, Heinsohn and Ramsey were gone. Only Russell was a bridge to the past, serving with John Havlicek, Sam Jones, Bailey Howell, Larry Siegfried and Don Nelson.

After finishing second to Philadelphia for the third straight year, the Celtics defeated Detroit, four games to two, and then met Philadelphia—and Wilt Chamberlain—in the semifinals. (Wilt had been traded by San Francisco in 1965.)

Boston and Philadelphia split the first six games of the series, so once again the seventh game was the crucial one. Boston was ahead in that contest, 97–95, with just 54 seconds remaining when Philadelphia's Wally Jones stole the ball and passed it to Chet Walker. Then Walker drove in for a lay-up, but his shot rolled off the rim. Russell grabbed the rebound, dribbled the length of the court and was fouled by Chamberlain as he got off the shot. Bill converted the free throw for a three-point play, and the Celtics won, 100–96. It was truly Russell's victory.

In *Sports Illustrated*, Frank Deford wrote: "Russell, as brilliant as ever, though thirty-four and in his twelfth pro year, restricted Chamberlain in a manner few believed possible. In the last half of the final, critical game, Wilt took only one shot and batted up only one errant attempt by a teammate."

The championship series against Los Angeles was almost anticlimactic, and the Celtics wrapped it up in six games. Laker Jerry West had high praise for the Celtics, especially Bill Russell. "They can talk about individual players in any sport," West said, "but I tell you, when it comes to winning there is no one like Bill Russell. This guy is the greatest of them all."

But great as he was, Bill was aging, and so were the Celtics. Teams like the New York Knicks and the Baltimore Bullets were making their moves to the top of the heap. Russell would be retiring in another year, and like Cousy, he wanted to leave pro basketball as a champion.

Russell wasn't even sure he wanted to play and coach the 1968–69 season, but it turned out to be the most dramatic year of all. Boston finished fourth in the Eastern Division, barely making the playoffs at all. But the Celtics found their old magic as soon as the playoffs began. No team had more experience under pressure, and as a result they eliminated Philadelphia in five games in the opening round.

New York, meanwhile, had knocked off the division champ, Baltimore, in four surprising games. Then, as the emotion and drama built, the Celtics drove past the Knicks in six games. Boston won the final, 106–105, on an "impossible" last-second shot by Havlicek, who was 20 feet away and off-balance when he simply lofted the ball toward the basket. It went in. As unlikely as it seemed, Boston was in the

Russell grabs a rebound during the 1969 playoffs against the Knicks. Other Celtics are John Havlicek (17), Don Nelson (19) and Sam Jones (24).

final. And again, the opponents wore Laker uniforms—but this year they had a new man in the pivot! It would be another classic match-up: the Celtics against the Lakers, Big Wilt against Big Bill.

Boston's chances seemed hopeless. The Lakers won the first game, 120–118, when West scored 53 points. They won the second game, 118–112, with 41 points from West and 32 from Baylor. But then Boston won the third game, 111–105.

Now it was the crucial fourth game. The Lakers could take a commanding three to one lead, or the Celtics could tie it up at two games each.

Game four was close all the way, and with 15 seconds remaining the Lakers had an 88–87 lead. It was a Laker ball, but a pass from Baylor to Johnny Egan was stolen by the Celtics' Emmette Bryant. Sam Jones tried a shot for Boston, but he missed. Wilt tapped the rebound to Baylor. But Elgin stepped out of bounds as he caught the ball, and with seven seconds to go the Celtics had time for just one play.

Bryant passed in-bounds to Havlicek. Havlicek passed to Sam Jones, who came around from the other corner of the court. Jones took the ball but bumped into teammate Bailey Howell as he jumped to shoot. Jones was off-balance but somehow, miraculously, the shot went in as the buzzer sounded. Boston had won the game, 89–88.

The Lakers came back to win the fifth game,

Big Wilt shoots over the outstretched arm of Russell as Boston and Los Angeles vie for the 1969 championship.

117–104, but Boston tied it again in the sixth game, 99–90.

Game seven was not only the final game of the series—it was the final game of Russell's long and glorious career. The game would be played in Los Angeles, which gave the Lakers an edge. But no one could take it away from Russell now. He had come too far and worked too hard. He wanted one more victory, one more championship.

It was a wild and exciting game. The score was tied at 60–60 early in the third quarter when the Lakers suddenly turned cold. They missed 15 straight shots and at the end of the period Boston held a 15-point lead.

The Celtics pulled ahead by 21 points in the first few minutes of the fourth quarter and looked like sure winners. But then the Lakers came storming back.

Boston's lead dwindled to 103–102. Then Wilt hurt his leg. Limping badly, he was taken out by coach Bill van Breda Kolff. He sat on the bench for a minute, then said he was ready to play again. But the coach thought the team would have more speed without Wilt in the game and decided not to send him back in.

With just seconds to go, Boston was ahead 108–106 when Mel Counts, the 7-footer who had replaced Wilt, got off a shot from almost under the basket that would have tied the game. But no one could take it away from Russell now. The big Celtic blocked the shot, and Bill Russell and company had their championship.

It was the proper way for Bill Russell to retire—as a champion!

Although Auerbach pleaded with him to reconsider, and to retire as a player but continue as coach, Russell wouldn't weaken.

"I'm not involved anymore," he told *Sports Illustrated*. "There are professionals and there are mercenaries in sports. The difference between them is that the professionals are involved. I won't play as a mercenary, and I won't coach as one. I played because I enjoyed it—because I was dedicated to being the best. Winning this last championship was one of the more rewarding victories of my career, especially because we weren't expected to win."

"To tell the truth," Russell added, "it's been a long time since I tried to prove anything to anybody. I know who I am, and with nothing left to prove, a lot of meaning has left sports for me."

It was certainly not the end of basketball for Russell. He moved back to California, settling in Los Angeles, and after a brief spell as an actor he signed a $100,000 contract with the ABC television network to announce the NBA games.

Russell's sound knowledge of the game, his unusual honesty and his high-pitched cackle enchanted millions of viewers. "I try not to say the things people expect me to say," he explained. "If it's a lousy game, I'll say so. Basketball is too important to me to lie about it. Every superstar I've ever known has played some lousy games. It's no disgrace, and it shouldn't be ignored or covered up by television announcers."

Bill was as outspoken off the air as on. A reporter once asked him how he thought he would have done against Kareem Abdul-Jabbar. To which Russell replied: "Young man, I think you have the question backwards."

And of course he was right. In the world of big men, Bill Russell was the first. He was there ahead of Chamberlain, and he had already retired when Abdul-Jabbar began to play with the Milwaukee Bucks.

Bill was the finest defensive center ever to play professional basketball. He made defense an art, and became a superstar without being a scoring champion. The point, according to Russell, was not to score, but to win.

When Kareem Abdul-Jabbar appeared in the NBA the season after Russell retired, Milwaukee coach Larry Costello said that the young center "combines the defensive skills of Bill Russell with the scoring potential of Wilt Chamberlain."

Wherever big men are measured, Bill Russell is remembered—the Celtic star is the standard against whom all others will be judged.

Wilt Chamberlain

Johnny Green of the Cincinnati Royals never forgot the first time he met Wilt Chamberlain on the basketball court. It was 1959 and Green was a rookie.

"Early in the game I blocked one of Wilt's shots," he recalled years later. "The crowd roared. When we were running back up the court, he smiled at me. When he got the ball again he just bulled his way to the basket and stuffed the ball down through the rim so hard that I knew my hand would have been broken if I had tried to block it.

"Then I realized something. When I blocked the first shot, he was about to stuff it through. But he felt me touch the ball and he just let it go easy. He didn't want to hurt me. I never forgot that—and I never tried to get him riled up again, either."

Green had met up with the most awesome player pro basketball had ever seen. In the following years, Wilt Chamberlain would set nearly every scoring record in the sport—most points in a game, most

points in a season, most points in a career, highest
season average and many more. He would also use
his tremendous height on defense, blocking count-
less shots and taking down record numbers of
rebounds.

Wilt established himself as the closest thing to a
one-man basketball team ever seen on the court—
and yet throughout most of his career he would be
known among his critics as a loser. People would
come by the thousands to see him play, but when his
team won they would say, "Any team with a man
that tall *should* win." When his team lost, however,
the fault was always his. Late in his career, Wilt
shrugged and summed up the fans' attitudes. "No
one loves a Goliath," he said.

Wilt Norman Chamberlain was born on August
21, 1936, in Philadelphia, Pennsylvania. His family
lived in an area called Haddington, a black ghetto on
the west side of the city.

There were nine children in the Chamberlain
family. Wilt never had many of the things other boys
had because his father worked as a handyman and
earned only $60 a week. Wilt's father was only
5-foot-10, and his mother was one inch shorter. But
his parents were not too surprised when their son
began to grow very tall, because Wilt's grandfather
had been nearly 7-feet tall and one of his older
brothers had grown to 6-foot-5.

As a youngster, Wilt was so much taller than the
other boys that he became terribly self-conscious.
He felt people were staring at him whenever he

walked down the street or went to school. Everything about his height saddened him.

When Wilt was only ten years old he earned a nickname that stuck with him for life. He was so tall even then that he was always bumping his head on doorways and low ceilings. His friends laughingly suggested that he "dip under" those areas, and when he did they began to call him "The Dipper." Wilt hated the teasing, but there was no other way he could avoid hitting his head.

At that time Wilt's favorite sports were handball, dodge-ball and porch-jumping. "What I liked best was porch-jumping," he recalled, "but I'm surprised I didn't get badly hurt doing it."

Porch-jumping was a game all the neighborhood boys played. On North Salford Street, where Wilt grew up, all the houses were two-story, attached buildings. Over the tiny front porch of each house was a small, slanted roof. Wilt would climb up to the roof over his porch and then jump from one to the next all the way down the block. Wilt also liked to run, and in the sixth grade he took part in many special races for the fastest boys in the city's schools.

All the while he was growing . . . and growing . . . and growing. During one summer he added four inches to his height! His father had to raise all the light fixtures in the house to save them—and his son's head.

When Wilt was 13 he was a student at Shoemaker Junior High School in Philadelphia. He was 6-foot-5. At the age of 16 he was a student at Overbrook High School—and he had grown to 6-foot-11.

But something even more important had happened in those three years. Wilt had learned to play basketball, and because he was so tall he played it better than any other boy in Philadelphia. Soon he was playing the game better than anyone his age in the United States.

Basketball became part of Wilt's life when he was 13 years old. Until then he had not played the game at all. But when the Philadelphia Department of Recreation built a neighborhood playground called Haddington Center near his home, he soon discovered he could play very well.

A lot of other people were discovering the same thing, and many of them wanted to help the young giant develop his skills. "Blinky" Brown, an older boy who also played at the center, remembers all the people who worked with Wilt. "No one man made Wilt a success," he said. "Many, many people contributed to his coaching, because we all saw how good he could become.

"We were proud of him, you know, because he was one of us—from our own neighborhood. One of the good things about him was that he'd always listen to his coaches. He'd listen carefully but he'd always make up his own mind, too. At first, he was a little too timid and he took a lot of punishment during a game because of that."

But Wilt learned quickly, and soon he was playing basketball as often as he could. He played in a church league, on a YMCA team, in the Police Athletic League and on a team that represented Haddington Center.

By the time he was ready to go to high school Wilt was an outstanding basketball player. He was still a track star, too, and set many national records for boys his age in the high jump and broad jump as well as in several running distances.

At Overbrook High School, Wilt's coach was Sam Cozen. Sam could see how good Wilt was—but even more important, he was able to see how good Wilt might become. The coach gave up much of his free time to work with the young giant.

"The big difference between Wilt and just another tall boy was that he was coordinated and agile," Cozen once said. "He had huge hands, and he knew all the tricks and angles in rebounding. He had great stamina, too. He could run all day and never get tired."

In his first year at Overbrook, Wilt was given another nickname when a Philadelphia sportswriter named Jack Ryan wrote, "Wilt has such spindly arms and pipestem legs that he looks like a man walking on stilts." From then on, Chamberlain was known as "Wilt the Stilt."

In his first varsity year Wilt led Overbrook to one victory after another. The undefeated players looked forward to the last game of the season—for the 1953 Pennsylvania State Championship. To win the title they would have to beat West Catholic High, and the confident Overbrook team expected little competition.

But West Catholic was not intimidated by the huge center. Its coach had spent hours preparing his players for Wilt. During practice sessions he put one

player on a table at the foul line and then had four others attempt to "guard" him by jumping up high in the air, waving their hands in his face and yelling at him.

The defense worked out just as the coach expected. Wilt was guarded by four opponents, leaving the rest of the Overbrook players open on the outside. Unfortunately, Wilt's teammates were unable to make many shots from the longer distances, and Overbrook lost the game.

That was the end of Wilt's sophomore season at Overbrook. It was also the last time his high school team lost a game.

The next year undefeated Overbrook again met West Catholic in the state finals. The West Catholic boys tried the same trick they had used the year before, but this time it didn't help much. Wilt scored 32 points in that game, and Overbrook won the championship.

"The only way to stop Wilt is to have him forget to show up for a game," Jack Ryan wrote. But Wilt did not forget, of course. He even found time to lead his Christian Street team to the national YMCA championship that year.

By the time he was a senior, Wilt was impossible to guard—and Overbrook was impossible to beat. Wilt led the school to another state championship, breaking every high school scoring record in Pennsylvania history along the way. Twice he scored 90

Already 6-foot-11, Wilt leaps too high for the ball during his days at Overbrook High School in Philadelphia.

points in a game, and in his three years of varsity
action he averaged 37 points per game.

By then, he had attracted national attention. In
1955 *Sport* Magazine did a story on him entitled
"The High School Kid Who Could Play Pro Basketball Now." That was no exaggeration, as a man
named Eddie Gottlieb realized. Gottlieb was the
owner of the Philadelphia Warriors, the team Wilt
always rooted for. Chamberlain hoped to play for
the Warriors some day—and Eddie Gottlieb wanted
to make sure that he would.

So before Wilt was even out of high school
Gottlieb persuaded the other NBA team owners to
agree to a new rule, which later became known as
"The Chamberlain Rule." The Warriors asked the
league to agree to a "territorial" draft of high school
players. According to this plan a pro team could
"claim" a player from its geographical territory
before he went away to college—and Eddie Gottlieb's Warriors would get the rights to Wilt Chamberlain.

Although every pro team would have liked to get
Wilt, the owners agreed to the plan. They realized
that other outstanding high school players were
bound to come out of their areas one day, and then
they would have the same advantage. So the Warriors drafted Wilt, and sat back to wait for the day
when this rare athlete would play for them.

But Wilt wasn't giving much thought to his pro
career at that time. He was having enough trouble
deciding which college to attend. Naturally, hundreds of schools wanted him to play basketball for

them. Every day he received many letters, telephone calls and even visits from college coaches and recruiters trying to convince the high school star to attend their schools. During his junior and senior years in high school Wilt spent just about every weekend visiting college campuses, looking around and talking to coaches and students.

Finally Wilt decided to accept the scholarship offer from the University of Kansas. It was a school rich in basketball tradition. In fact, the man who invented the game of basketball, Dr. James Naismith, had once been the school's athletic director. Wilt was also impressed with Kansas' basketball coach, "Phog" Allen, who was then in his 39th year of coaching. Allen had won more games than any other college coach in history. He was kindly, almost fatherly, and Wilt liked him right away.

Of course, many of the colleges which did not succeed in getting Wilt were disappointed. Some even accused Kansas of giving Wilt a lot of money to help him make up his mind. Some professionals also thought Wilt had been given money. Walter Brown, the owner of the Boston Celtics, said: "I don't know what the figure is, but it is a matter of fact that no one in the NBA can afford to pay Chamberlain what he gets at Kansas!"

Those charges were false, however. All Wilt received was the cost of his room and board, tuition and books—and $15 each month, which he earned by selling programs at the Kansas football games.

As soon as the school year began, Wilt knew he had made the right choice. He was happy with the

Chamberlain makes his varsity debut with the University of Kansas team in 1956.

university, and the students treated him like a hero. He had a specially-made, 7-foot-6 bed in his room, and for the first time in his life Wilt (who had grown to 7-foot-1 by then) could sleep comfortably.

More important, Wilt finally discovered the benefits of his great height. "Being tall has given me an education and it will get me all the other things I want," he said. "Now I think I'm very lucky to be this big."

His freshman year was filled with fun. He joined a fraternity, and his roommate Charlie Tidwell was a track star at the university. Wilt tried out for the track team and became a star there, too. In 1958 he set a record with a high jump of 6-feet-3¼ inches in the Midwest's Big Eight Conference.

But Wilt's favorite sport was still basketball, and Wilt was Kansas' favorite player. A huge crowd turned out to watch his first game, which wasn't really a game at all but a practice session against the varsity team. The Kansas freshmen were not allowed to play on the varsity, so they had their own team. The freshmen beat the varsity, 81–71, and 42 of those points belonged to Chamberlain.

The freshmen did not play a regular schedule of games during the season. Mostly they played practice games or scrimmages, against the varsity or among themselves. But every time the freshmen and the varsity met, the freshmen came out on top. The school's best varsity players were no match for Wilt.

Finally the year passed and Wilt was a sophomore, eligible for varsity basketball. The team had a new coach, a man named Dick Harp, who was hired when 70-year-old Phog Allen decided to retire. It was a very difficult decision for the old coach to make. "I waited all my life to coach someone like Wilt," he explained, "but my health just wouldn't allow it."

Kansas' first game of the 1956–57 season attracted more than 15,000 fans. It was Wilt's first real game, and everyone wanted to be able to say, "I was there." No one was disappointed, either. Kansas beat Northwestern University, 87–69, as Wilt scored 52 points and took down 31 rebounds.

Wilt was so good he was frightening. No one could cover him, and no one could shoot over him. In fact, right after his first game the National Collegiate Athletic Association (the NCAA) announced two new rules.

The first rule made it illegal for the foul shooter to cross the foul line until the ball hit either the rim or the backboard. Wilt was so good that he could take his free shot and if it missed, leap toward the hoop to tap it in. When he did this the basket would count as a two-point field goal instead of a one-point foul shot.

The second rule prevented a player from guiding a teammate's shot into the basket. Wilt's fantastic size allowed him to stand under the basket when one of his teammates took a shot, then reach up and "direct" the ball down through the hoop for two points. Today this is known as offensive goaltending, and it is still illegal.

But the new "Chamberlain rules" didn't come close to stopping Wilt. There were never less than two men guarding him, sometimes three and often four. But even that didn't really help. Something else had to be done if any other team expected to beat Kansas.

Coach Bill Strannigan of Iowa State finally did something. He put his 6-foot-9 center behind Wilt, his two forwards in front of him and told his two guards to chase the other Kansas players and make them hurry their shots. His offensive strategy was just as well thought out. Strannigan had his team hold the ball without trying to shoot until someone could work free for a sure shot. The "slowdown" game was successful, and Iowa State beat Kansas, 39–37.

It was the first game Kansas had lost with Wilt, and the upset surprised everyone. Newspapers all across the country announced the defeat with banner headlines. But two weeks later the same teams met again, and this time Wilt was ready. He did the one thing Iowa State never expected. He moved away from under the basket, which opened up the lane for his teammates to take driving lay-ups. Kansas won that game, and it was Wilt's unselfishness that made it possible.

With only one defeat, Kansas easily became the champion of the Big Eight and earned a place in the postseason NCAA tournament to determine the national champion. Kansas won its three preliminary games, beating Southern Methodist University, Oklahoma City University and the University of San Francisco. Finally there were just two teams left in the tournament—Kansas and North Carolina.

The night they played for the national championship was a memorable one. The North Carolina coach, Frank McGuire, devised a defense similar to the one that Iowa State had used. North Carolina also had a fine offense with some great shooters. It was the best team Kansas had met all season. But then Kansas was the best team North Carolina had played.

The game was exciting and closely fought, and it did not end until the teams had played three overtime periods. North Carolina finally won, 54–53. It was another upset and just the second loss of the season for Kansas. But Wilt had been so good he was named the Most Valuable Player of the entire tournament.

By the start of his junior year, all of Kansas' rivals were using the slowdown they had learned from Iowa State and North Carolina. They all held the ball. They all assigned three men to cover Wilt. And they all tried to foul him because strangely enough super-scorer Wilt was not a good free-throw shooter.

The teams did manage to keep Wilt from scoring a lot of points, but he was so good that Kansas finished the season with an 18–5 record anyway. The games became much less exciting, though, and Wilt was very unhappy.

Then Wilt shocked every fan in the country by quitting college, even though he still had one more year to go. His story appeared in *Look* Magazine on June 10, 1958. The headline read: "Why I Am

Wilt snatches a rebound out of the hands of Oklahoma City's Roger Holloway.

Quitting College." In the article Wilt complained that he couldn't play the kind of basketball he loved because other teams wouldn't let him.

"The game I was forced to play at Kansas was not basketball," he wrote. "It was hurting my chances of ever developing into a successful pro. I will make a barnstorming tour which will give me a chance to play some real basketball and give me a chance to make some money so I can help out my family. I want them to enjoy life more, and the only way I could ever help them is through the dollar value of my basketball ability."

In the middle of the summer Chamberlain joined the Harlem Globetrotters, the most famous "barnstorming" basketball team in the world.

All the Globetrotters were black players. The team was named after the best-known black area in the country, New York City's Harlem, but the players came from all over the United States. They were professionals, but unlike the players in the NBA, they clowned around and entertained fans with fancy dribbling, trick plays and "show business" acts. They even took along a team of other players on most trips, and before each game the two teams decided just how the Globetrotters were going to win.

Abe Saperstein, a white man from Chicago, had founded the Globetrotters and become a millionaire because of their success. Saperstein was able to hire some of the best black basketball players in the United States, but the man he really wanted was Wilt Chamberlain. The two most famous players on the Globetrotters—Goose Tatum and Marques Haynes—had just retired. The only star left was a younger man named Meadowlark Lemon, and the Globetrotters wanted another big "name" player on the team.

Wilt insisted on a lot of money, and Saperstein was willing to pay it. When he signed his contract in July of 1958, newspapers predicted that Chamberlain would earn $65,000 for the next year. The first thing Wilt did with his money was to buy a house for his parents. Then he set out to become the most famous player the Globetrotters ever had.

Wilt played guard with the team. Imagine, a guard who was 7-foot-1! The fans were so eager to see Wilt dribble, pass, score and rebound that there was seldom an empty seat at a Globetrotter game. All tickets were usually sold long before the Globetrotters came to town.

Wilt joined the team in Italy and became an instant sensation. From Italy the team toured the rest of Europe. The Globetrotters played in France, Austria, Germany and England.

By autumn the Globetrotters had returned home to the United States. In October, Wilt played his first game in New York City's Madison Square Garden, and more than 18,000 people came to see him. One official of the Garden said, "We had so many requests for tickets we could have sold out Yankee Stadium."

Wilt the Stilt, the Harlem Globetrotters' 7-foot-1 guard, dribbles toward teammate Goose Tatum. ▶

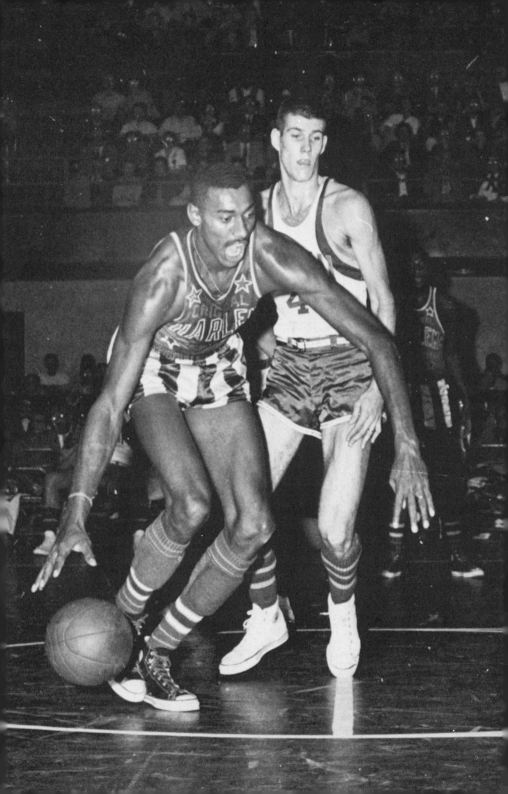

The Globetrotters won that game, bringing their record for the year to 411–0! They averaged nearly eight games a week all year long—and they never lost!

Wilt enjoyed all the excitement, and he learned a lot by playing almost every day. But playing for the Globetrotters wasn't all fun and games. The team was always on the go, always traveling someplace. Many of the games were in the smaller cities and towns, so often the only way the Globetrotters could travel was by bus. That was especially uncomfortable for a fellow as big as Wilt. The players had to eat many of their meals at strange hours, so they often had nothing but sandwiches and soda pop on the buses.

In April of 1959, Wilt's contract with the Globetrotters expired and he decided to leave the team. Saperstein was upset because in the nine months Wilt had been his star, business had increased by 20 percent. As a favor he asked Wilt to make one final trip with the Globetrotters—to Russia.

So that summer Wilt went to Russia with the Globetrotters. There he met Nikita Khrushchev, who was then the Russian premier and one of the most powerful men in the world. Even *he* wanted to see the famous Wilt Chamberlain.

Looking back at his year with the Globetrotters, Wilt remembered it as the greatest time of his life. He forgot the long bus rides, the cold meals and the lonely times away from his family. The Globetrotters had given him the chance to play a lot of basketball —and make a lot of money. It was just as he had planned. The constant play had made him stronger and faster. Wilt Chamberlain was ready for the NBA.

Naturally, his team would be the Philadelphia Warriors. And did they ever need him! The Warriors had finished in last place in 1958–59, winning only 32 games and losing 40. They had not even made the playoffs, and only one other club in the eight-team league had been left out.

The Warriors were thrilled to have Chamberlain on the team, and they gave him the best contract anyone in the league had ever received. Until Wilt signed his contract, the most any NBA player had ever earned was $25,000 a year. Chamberlain signed for nearly twice that amount.

The Warriors considered it a bargain. With Wilt's help they would be a good, strong team. They already had Paul Arizin, a fine scorer and playmaker; Woody Sauldsberry, a strong rebounder; Guy Rodgers, a great ball handler; and Tom Gola and Joe Grabowski, two solid forwards.

What the Warriors had needed all along was a big center who could score and rebound. After waiting four years, finally they had him—Wilt Chamberlain, the best of them all.

Their huge rookie was everything the Warriors had hoped he would be. Wilt's first NBA game was against the New York Knicks. It was played in Madison Square Garden, the Knicks' home court and the same arena Wilt had filled just a year earlier as the star of the Globetrotters.

Wilt didn't disappoint anyone in the crowd of 18,000—except those who had wanted to see the Knicks win. He scored 43 points. He made 17 of his

20 shots. He had 28 rebounds. He blocked twelve New York shots. He was just terrific!

There was another super-center in the NBA then, Bill Russell of the league-leading Boston Celtics. Everyone was anxious to see their first meeting. And when it happened, it was all that people expected.

Wilt scored 30 points and Russell 22. But Russell pulled down 38 rebounds to Wilt's 35. Both men played a great game, but the Celtics won by a score of 115–106.

Afterwards, Russell had high praise for Chamberlain. "I have played against men this big but never against anyone this big and this strong and this good," he said. "You just can't relax for a second. He's the best rookie ever."

Somebody asked another member of the Celtics, Gene Conley, how to stop Wilt. "About the only thing you can do is lock the door to the dressing room before he gets out," Conley said, laughing. "Once he gets to the court, there's nothing anybody can do."

Philadelphia finished the 1959–60 season second in the Eastern Division and went into the playoffs. In the first round they beat a star-filled Syracuse team which included Dolph Schayes, John Kerr, Hal Greer and Larry Costello.

Then the Warriors played the Celtics for the Eastern Conference championship. It was time for another Chamberlain–Russell duel.

Surrounded by New York Knicks, Wilt is fouled by Johnny Green (11) in a 1960 game.

Boston won the first game 111–105. In the second game Wilt got into a fight with Boston's Tom Heinsohn and hurt his hand. It bothered him for the rest of the playoffs, and the Celtics won in six games.

In the sixth game the score was tied 117–117 with eleven seconds left to play. Then Philadelphia's Guy Rodgers missed two free throws—and the chance to win it for the Warriors. Russell got the rebound and moments later Heinsohn leaped for the basket and tapped the ball in just as the buzzer sounded, giving Boston a 119–117 win.

It was a great victory for the Celtics. Not only had they beaten the Warriors, they had beaten Wilt Chamberlain. Still, Wilt had scored 50 points in the fifth game—with a sore hand.

Even without the championship it had been a good year for the Warriors and a spectacular one for Wilt. During the regular season Chamberlain set records by the truckload. Among the more outstanding were his 37.6 points-per-game average, his 2,707 total points, his 26.9 rebounds per game, his 2,311 field-goal attempts and his 1,065 field goals.

Wilt was named the NBA's Rookie of the Year, Most Valuable Player and first-team center on the All-Star team. His value to the league didn't stop there, though. During his rookie season, the NBA's attendance figures went up 24 percent, and one league official admitted that Wilt was probably responsible for all of it.

Wilt leaps up to put one over Bill Russell as the Celtics and Warriors meet in the 1960 Eastern playoff finals.

Wilt Chamberlain did the same thing for basketball that super-slugger Babe Ruth had done for baseball. He gave the fans a larger-than-life hero. When Wilt came to town people clamored for tickets to see him play. Many of those people would not have come to an NBA game the year before if the tickets were free!

It seemed the only person who wasn't happy with his first season was Wilt himself. In another magazine article, he criticized the league's rules: "The NBA has two standards for officiating—one for me and one for the rest of the league."

Wilt was upset because he believed other teams were using a "zone defense" to guard him with more than one man even though zone defenses were not allowed in the NBA. Wilt also resented the rough style of play other teams used against him. Elbows were swung at him all season, and after being hit by one such blow Wilt had to have two teeth extracted.

He was so upset that he shocked the NBA by announcing his retirement! The Warriors pleaded with him to stay, and Wilt finally changed his mind.

The next season (1960–61) was a good one for Wilt but a disappointing one for the Warriors. They were second to Boston again and then were eliminated in the first round of the playoffs.

During the regular season Wilt scored a total of 3,033 points for a 38.3-point-per-game average, and once more he led the league in rebounding, too. But again there were problems. During the season Wilt had frequent arguments with Warrior coach Neil Johnston, a former star of the team. Finally Eddie

Gottlieb decided that the Warriors needed a change and replaced Johnston with a new coach for the 1961–62 season. He picked Frank McGuire, the man whose North Carolina University team had beaten Wilt's Kansas University team in the NCAA tournament years ago.

Even with their new coach, the Warriors still played badly at times. But that didn't stop Wilt from having an unbelievable year. He scored a total of 4,029 points that season, which averaged out to 50.4 points per game. During one stretch in February of 1962 he scored 451 points in eight games—with individual games of 78, 61, 55, 52, 43, 50, 57 and 55.

But Wilt's most incredible game took place on March 2, 1962, against the New York Knicks. In the first quarter Wilt made seven of 14 field-goal shots and nine of nine free throws for 23 points. In the second period he made seven of twelve field goals and four of five foul shots for another 18 points. That gave him a 41-point total by half time.

During the intermission coach McGuire told the team to pass the ball to Wilt. "Chamberlain is getting free underneath the basket," he said, "so let's keep giving him the shots."

In the third period Wilt took 16 shots and made ten. He made all eight free throws he took. That added up to 28 third-quarter points.

By now the fans in the arena knew Wilt had scored 69 points, and everyone was wondering if he could make it 100. To do that, he would have to score 31 points in the fourth quarter.

When he realized he was going for a new league

scoring record, Chamberlain really started steaming. With just 42 seconds to play Wilt had made eleven of 20 field goals and seven of ten free throws. He had 98 points! Philadelphia had the ball, and Guy Rodgers passed it to Paul Arizin. Arizin lofted a high pass to Wilt underneath the basket. Chamberlain jumped up to catch it, and on the way down he stuffed the ball into the basket for one of his famous dunk shots.

It was the most exciting dunk he ever made. The final score was Philadelphia 169, New York 147— Chamberlain 100. Wilt had set an NBA record that would not be broken easily.

The second-highest scorer on the team that game was a rookie from Newark, New Jersey, named Alvin Attles. He scored 17 points. Attles, who later became head coach of the Golden State Warriors, remembered that game clearly: "I always knew how good Wilt was, and I always knew how much better than anyone else he could be, but I never thought anyone, not even Wilt Chamberlain, could score that many points in one game. Just playing in that game was the highlight of my career."

Because of Wilt's great scoring, Philadelphia ended the season with a strong rally and finished second to the Celtics again. The Warriors beat Syracuse in the first round of the 1962 playoffs, and once again they found themselves going against the Celtics for the Eastern Conference championship.

It was a wild, exciting series, which went the full seven games. Boston finally won on a shot by Sam Jones—just two seconds before the end of the final game. It was a rough series, too. In the fifth game Wilt got into an argument with Jones, a much smaller man. Sam said something that made Wilt furious, and the giant center began to chase after him. Jones ran to the Boston bench, picked up a small stool and held it over his head either as a weapon or a shield—he wasn't sure which.

A photographer happened to catch a picture of Sam holding the stool while Wilt stalked him, and it

Chamberlain takes a giant step to grab a rebound from Boston's Satch Sanders.

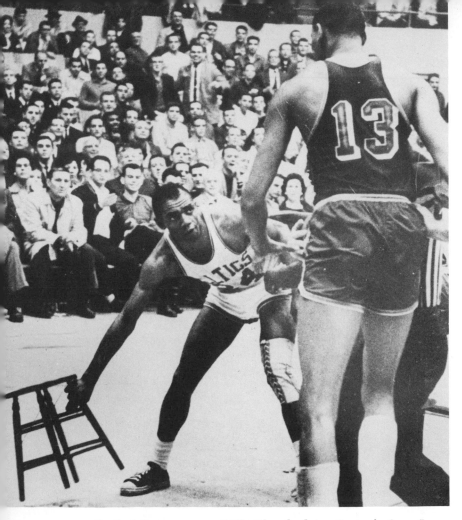

Stalked by an angry Wilt Chamberlain, Boston's Sam Jones reaches for a stool in self-defense.

was published in hundreds of newspapers. Because of his size, the picture made Chamberlain look like a bully—and a foolish one at that. "I can't even get angry and lose my temper like other men," he complained. "Whatever I do is either not enough or too much."

The 1962–63 season began a new era for Wilt and

the Warriors. The Philadelphia fans, tired of too many second-place finishes and playoff losses to Boston, hadn't been buying enough tickets, and the team was losing money. So the Warriors moved clear across the country to San Francisco.

The move to California put the Warriors in the Western Division of the NBA, so they finally escaped the Celtics. Moving forced another change, too. Frank McGuire did not want to leave the East, and he resigned as head coach. The Warriors hired a man named Bob Feerick, a former NBA player and coach at California's Santa Clara College.

Despite the big changes it was not a happy season. Paul Arizin had quit, not wanting to move to San Francisco, and the Warriors did not have any good rookies that year. But they still had Wilt. He scored more points than anyone in the league again—3,586 for a 44.8-per-game average. And he was the NBA rebounding leader again, too.

After all that, though, the Warriors finished a disappointing fourth in the five-team Western Division and failed to reach the playoffs. To make matters worse, Wilt had been goaded into many more brawls, and the fans were becoming critical of the San Francisco star. They claimed he was selfish, taking all the shots himself. It was not a pleasant situation. Finally, Feerick was dismissed and a new coach was hired. He was a man who would change Wilt's life, his style of basketball and his attitude. His name was Alex Hannum.

Hannum had played NBA basketball and had also been head coach of the St. Louis Hawks and the

Syracuse Nationals. He had firm ideas about "team basketball." He insisted that the open man get the pass and take the shot, and he considered a good defense to be at least as important as a good offense.

Shortly after Hannum took over, he made a dramatic announcement. "Wilt Chamberlain must change his style of play," the new coach said. "He must pass the ball more often, play more defense and take fewer shots."

Hannum also said that the other players on the team had come to depend too much on Wilt, so much so that they had forgotten how to play basketball themselves. Not surprisingly, the players disagreed, so Hannum decided to prove his point. He had the veterans scrimmage against a team of inexperienced rookies—with Wilt sitting on the bench. The rookies won the "game" easily.

Hannum had made his point, but many of the players were still not happy. Some felt that by limiting Wilt's shooting, the coach was wasting their best weapon. But soon his style of team play began to show results, and the Warriors got off to a good start in 1963–64. They won the Western Division championship with a 48–32 record. Even though he took less than half his usual number of shots, Wilt still led the NBA scoring with an average of 36.9 points per game.

By the end of the season the Warriors were winning the close games. They had never been able to do that before, because if a game was close the other teams knew the ball would be passed to Wilt. That meant they could concentrate their defense around the big center. Now they had to guard everyone. Therefore, it was easier for any one Warrior to work himself clear.

In the first round of the playoffs, the Warriors were pitted against the tough St. Louis Hawks. The Hawks had one of the league's all-time great players, a 6-foot-9 forward named Bob Pettit, and an outstanding rookie forward named Zelmo Beaty. It was a very close, exciting series. The Warriors finally won it in seven games and prepared to go into the finals. That contest had the whole country excited.

Once more the Warriors would face the Boston Celtics, their former rivals in the Eastern Division. And once more the league's two best centers, Wilt Chamberlain and Bill Russell, would meet.

Wilt was asked a lot of questions about Russell before the series began. He told everyone of his great respect for the Celtic star and then went on to say, "Russell has great professional abilities, but I feel that if he had been with another team, he would have had to be a different type of player. The Celtics have so many great shooters that Bill has been able to concentrate on defense and rebounding. With another team he might have had to produce as a scorer, too, and he would not have become known as a defensive specialist."

There was a bit of a sting to that "compliment"— and a little envy, too. Wilt always felt he was as good a defensive player as Russell, maybe even better. But throughout his career he'd had to be his team's high scorer, too.

The playoff series was a disappointment to Wilt

and the Warriors. Boston won the first two games when the other Warriors had trouble making outside shots. When his teammates started to feed the ball to Wilt, the Celtics gave him the old "treatment," fouling and pushing the big center. In the second game Wilt got so angry with the way Boston's Clyde Lovellette was fouling him that he punched the bulky reserve center. The 6-foot-9, 250-pound center flew through the air and landed flat on his back.

All the Warriors could do was win one game, the third, and after five games Boston was again the NBA champion.

The 1964–65 season was distressing for Wilt. He missed the first two months of the season when he was hospitalized for a serious stomach disorder, and by the time he was ready to play again he found himself out of shape. Soon he was injured, too, and the Warriors found themselves struggling in last place without their big center. Wilt wasn't the Warriors' only worry. It was beginning to look as though they had made a mistake by moving to San Francisco. The fans weren't buying tickets, so the team was losing not only games but a lot of money, too. Something had to be done.

The Warriors finally came up with a solution to their problems, but it was so extreme that no one could believe it. At the 1965 All-Star game in St. Louis, the Warriors announced that they had traded Wilt Chamberlain back to Philadelphia—where a

St. Louis' Phil Jordan has his hand up through the basket as he loses a rebound to Wilt.

new team called the 76ers had taken the place of the Warriors.

The management admitted that what they really wanted to "trade" was Wilt's big contract because they could no longer afford to pay him. In return for Wilt, the Warriors received three other players (Connie Dierking, Lee Shaffer and Paul Neumann) plus almost $100,000 in cash.

The Philadelphia fans were overjoyed. Their new team had not been playing very well, despite the presence of such stars as Hal Greer, Chet Walker, Larry Costello and Luke Jackson. The 76ers were then in third place, and the fans were not coming out to their games.

Chamberlain's first game "back home" was a sellout. He received a standing ovation from his fans, and the 76ers won the game easily. With Wilt's help they continued to win, taking nine of their next eleven games. By the time the regular season ended the 76ers had fought their way up to a 40–40 record, and they had made the playoffs.

Cincinnati, their first opponent, fell quickly. Then, to everyone's delight, the 76ers prepared to play the Celtics again. But this time it looked like a different story. Sparked by Wilt, the 76ers split the first six games. Then came the final, seventh game, one of the most exciting in playoff history.

With two minutes left to play, Boston had a 110–103 lead. Then Wilt scored six straight points, and with six seconds to go it was suddenly 110–109. The Celtics tried to put the ball in play, but Wilt was guarding the in-bounds passer and forced him to throw the ball wildly. It hit the rim of the Philadelphia basket and bounced out of bounds.

The 76ers had the ball under the Philadelphia basket, but this time their in-bounds pass was batted away by Boston's John Havlicek. Time ran out before anyone could retrieve the ball, and the Celtics had won still another series from Wilt's team. It was, after all, the same old story with the same old ending.

Still, the 76ers were a powerful club. The next season (1965–66) they finished first in the Eastern Division, winning their last eleven games and ending the Celtics' nine-year streak as division champions. Once again Wilt led the NBA in scoring and rebounding and was voted the Most Valuable Player in the league.

The Celtics did it again in the playoffs, though, beating the 76ers in five games. But Russell, for one, was impressed with the "new" Wilt.

"He's a lot tougher these days," Russell said. "Before, when he got the ball, we knew he'd shoot. He had to, to keep his team in the game. But now he passes so often that he makes us hesitate."

In 1966–67, Philadelphia was determined not to be stopped again. And when the owners fired coach Dolph Schayes and brought in Alex Hannum, there was great hope for the season. Hannum had already proved he could work with Wilt, and now he had a fine collection of other players, too.

The whole season was right out of a fairy tale. Nothing went wrong. The 76ers won their first seven games, beating Boston in one of them by 42 points.

Playing with the Philadelphia 76ers in 1967, Wilt tangles with San Francisco's Nate Thurmond under the basket.

One loss was followed by eight more victories. Then came another loss. Then eight more victories. Wilt was playing Bill Russell's game now—defense, rebounding and screening for his teammates to let them take easy jump shots.

The Philadelphia fans fell in love with the team, and attendance at 76er home games nearly doubled that year. Most of the reason, of course, was Wilt and the team's wonderful winning record. But the owners had also collected a lot of "local" players who were already city heroes. Wally Jones and Bill Melchionni had played college basketball at Philadelphia's Villanova, and Matt Guokas had been a college star at St. Joseph's, also in Philly. And, of course, Wilt himself first attracted attention as a high school star in the city.

Halfway through the season the 76ers were 39–4, and they finished with a league record of 68 victories and only 13 defeats. To top it all off, Philadelphia clinched the division championship in a game against Boston. The Celtics had a 15-point lead when the 76ers rallied late in the game. With just six seconds to play, Wilt tied the score at 102–102 with a tap-in, forcing the game into an overtime period. In the overtime Greer scored on a 25-foot jump shot with two seconds to go for the Philadelphia victory. It was sweet revenge for the 76ers.

Now it was playoff time again, and with high hopes Philadelphia went into the first round against the Cincinnati Royals. The 76ers lost the first game, but then they won the next four to reach the Eastern finals.

The opponent? Boston. The result? Philadelphia won it in five quick games, taking the last one, 140–116. Wilt was at his best in that series, completely outplaying Russell.

In the five games, Chamberlain had 160 rebounds to Russell's 117. He had 50 assists to Russell's 30. And he had 108 points to Russell's 57.

After the fifth and final game Russell walked into the 76er locker room, still in his uniform. He had come to congratulate Wilt.

"Great game," said Russell.

"Thanks, baby," rumbled Wilt.

"Just great," Russell said.

"Right, baby," answered Wilt.

Then they shook hands and Russell left.

Now it was on to the championship. This time the 76ers' opposition was Chamberlain's old San Francisco team. The Warriors had regrouped and improved since Wilt had left. They had two big stars, Rick Barry and Nate Thurmond.

The 76ers won the first two games, but San Francisco won the third when Barry scored 55 points. Philadelphia won the fourth game and San Francisco the fifth.

Then came game six. The championship was in reach. With just a few seconds left the 76ers held a 123–122 lead, but San Francisco had the ball. Barry took a pass and started to drive. Wilt came out to menace him, leaving Thurmond free underneath the basket. Barry saw this and decided to pass to the big center, but Wilt was ready for that move. He quickly slid back and blocked Barry's passing lane.

Barry, already up in the air, was left hanging there. He had to force a desperate, off-balance shot. Barry's shot missed, the buzzer sounded and the 76ers were NBA champions!

Wilt was a winner. Ironically, something Wilt said showed just how much he had come to accept Hannum's "five-man" philosophy. "It is easier to play a team that has one man do most of the shooting," Wilt explained, referring to Barry and the Warriors. He seemed to have forgotten that three years before he had been the one man doing most of the shooting for his team—the same San Francisco Warriors.

The 76ers won the division again in 1967–68 and beat the New York Knicks in the first round of the playoffs. Then they found themselves playing—who else?—the Celtics for the Eastern championship.

The series went the full seven games. In the last match the Celtics were ahead, 97–95, with 34 seconds to play. Then Russell made one foul shot, and it was 98–95. In a scramble for a loose ball, Wilt and Boston's Don Nelson both got there at the same time, and the officials called for a jump ball. Wilt tapped it to the 76ers' Chet Walker, who drove in for a sure lay-up. But Russell blocked it.

Hal Greer grabbed the rebound and shot again, but the ball rolled around the rim and fell off. Then Russell took the next rebound, passed it to Sam Jones, who drew a foul and then made both free throws, giving Boston a five-point lead. The Celtics had another victory—and the 76ers had another disappointment.

That summer, the Philadelphia 76ers decided to trade Wilt to the Los Angeles Lakers. The Philadelphia fans were stunned and shocked, but Wilt just shrugged his huge shoulders and set out for Los Angeles. He knew what talent the Lakers had, and he knew he was the one man they needed to become a great team.

In return for Wilt, the 76ers received Archie Clark, Darrall Imhoff and Jerry Chambers—none of whom lasted very long in Philadelphia. Wilt became the top man for the Lakers and five seasons later he was still top man.

Chamberlain has the ball—and Don Nelson's head—as Philadelphia and Boston meet in the 1968 playoffs.

His move to Los Angeles was the start of a whole new chapter in Chamberlain's career. When he joined the Lakers, Wilt became the teammate of two of the most sensational scorers in the history of the NBA—Jerry West and Elgin Baylor. Many people expected problems because all three players liked to shoot.

But Wilt simply played the kind of basketball he had learned from Alex Hannum. He became the rebounder, the defensive giant and the shot-blocker, leaving the scoring to West and Baylor. The team was in a hurry to win. Since coming to Los Angeles in 1960, the Lakers had almost always had a good team—but not quite good enough. During those years they had played in more final series than any other team, but had never won a championship. The fans were getting impatient.

Now that they had Wilt as well as West and Baylor, they expected a championship. The three superstars felt the pressure. "When Wilt joined the Lakers," said West, "he, Elgin and I had each passed the age of thirty, had each been in the league nine or ten years, were set in our ways and fixed in our opinions, were breaking in with a brand new bunch of players and yet were under the pressure of being expected to produce miracles. It was an uneasy situation."

The Lakers didn't play as if they had troubles, though. Even when West injured his hand and missed 21 games, Los Angeles sailed along in first place and finished the season with 55 victories. Wilt played great defense, averaging more than 20 rebounds—and 20 points—each game.

In the playoffs the Lakers lost the first two games to San Francisco and then won the next four. Then they crushed the Atlanta Hawks to clinch the Western Division championship, winning four games to one.

And again, after another long season, Wilt found himself in a championship series—against the Boston Celtics.

Los Angeles won the first two games, and it looked as if their championship dreams might finally come true. The Celtics rallied to win the third and fourth games, but the Lakers took a three-to-two edge with a fifth-game victory. Then Boston scratched back once more to win the sixth game and tie up the series. The seventh game would tell the story.

During the first half it looked like anyone's game, but in the third period the Lakers seemed to fall apart. In the fourth quarter the Celtics put on the pressure and moved far out in front. But the Lakers came back to cut a 21-point deficit down to one. Then Wilt hurt his leg and, limping badly, left the game. A minute later Wilt asked to go back in, but Laker coach Bill van Breda Kolff felt the team was "hot" and didn't want to break up the five-man combination that was still going strong.

For a moment it looked as if the coach was right. The man substituting for Wilt, 7-foot Mel Counts, went in for a lay-up, but Russell blocked it and the game ended with Boston still on top.

Wilt had sat on the bench as the Lakers lost another championship. In the locker room West cried, and Wilt refused to talk to anyone.

When Bill Russell's retirement was announced after the playoffs, it seemed that 1969–70 would surely be Wilt's season. The Lakers got off to a good start and reached the final round of the playoffs. They went to seven games again, and they lost the championship again—this time to the New York Knicks.

In the 1970–71 season the Lakers won their division. But then West suffered a knee injury and was lost for the playoffs. Los Angeles fell to Mil-

waukee and young Kareem Abdul-Jabbar in the Western Conference championship.

Frustration was one word the Lakers lived with. Disappointment was another. Wilt had been playing in the NBA for 13 seasons, and his teams had won only one championship in all those years. "Wilt may be a great player," said his critics, "but he's a loser—and so are the Lakers."

But in the 1971–72 season Wilt and the Lakers lost all those labels. The only word for them was great. Los Angeles had another new coach. He was Bill Sharman, the former Celtic star and teammate of "winner" Bill Russell. Sharman, a no-nonsense coach, got right down to business. He made the players practice every day, even when they were going to play a game that night. He told Wilt that the season was in his hands.

Sharman then decided on a new starting line-up. Baylor had retired early in the season, so the Lakers needed another forward to go along with Happy Hairston. Sharman chose a young man named Jim McMillian, who had been an All-America player at Columbia University in New York City. The Lakers had traded Dick Garrett to the Buffalo Braves, so they also needed another guard. Sharman made a trade with the Phoenix Suns and came up with another All-America, Gail Goodrich from UCLA.

The starting line-up was complete. On the bench were such fine reserves as Leroy Ellis, Pat Riley,

Now a Laker, Wilt makes a tough off-balance shot in the 1969 playoff finals as Celtic Bill Russell (6) looks on.

Keith Erickson, Flynn Robinson and Willie Mc-Carter. Everybody knew it was a good team, but no one knew just how good it would turn out to be.

Sharman made Wilt the team captain because he was the player most respected by the rest of the Lakers. It was a smart move by Sharman, who had played on many championship Celtic teams and knew the value of team leadership. Wilt took his responsibility seriously. He was never late for meetings or practices, and he never complained about the hard work Sharman's system demanded.

In October the Lakers won a game—and then another—and still another. They did nothing but win all through November and December. By January they had won 33 games in a row, the longest winning streak by any team in the history of all professional sports.

Looking for their 34th win, the Lakers faced the Milwaukee Bucks. It was Milwaukee's record of 20 consecutive victories that the Lakers had broken, so the Bucks were hoping to be the ones to finally beat them.

The nationally televised game was played on a Sunday afternoon, and millions of fans watched Milwaukee win, 120–104.

But the Lakers could not be stopped by a lone defeat. They went on to win 69 games that season to set another record. It broke the record of 68 wins set by Wilt's Philadelphia team in 1966–67.

Chamberlain comes down with a rebound—onto the hip of Milwaukee's Kareem Abdul-Jabbar.

Other Laker records in 1971–72 included: most victories on the road, 31; most victories at home, 38; most games over 100 points, 81; highest winning percentage, .841; and largest margin of a single game victory, 63 points.

When the playoffs began, the Lakers were favored to win it all, and for a change they did. First they beat the Chicago Bulls in four straight games. Then for the Western Conference championship they had to play powerful Milwaukee. The Bucks were led by their giant center, Kareem Abdul-Jabbar, and one of the best guards in basketball history, Oscar Robertson. But the Lakers won in six games, thanks largely to Wilt.

Bill Russell, who by then had retired and become a television sports announcer, explained just how good Wilt was in his match with Abdul-Jabbar. "The Lakers are afraid of Kareem," he said, "but the Bucks are absolutely terrified and intimidated by Wilt."

Playing against Abdul-Jabbar, Wilt was superb. In the third game, for instance, he held the giant Buck scoreless for a twelve-minute stretch during the second and third quarters, blocking five of his shots.

In the fourth game Wilt prevented Kareem from scoring a single field goal in the final eleven minutes, and the Lakers won by three points. Then in the decisive sixth game Wilt blocked twelve shots, five of them by Abdul-Jabbar. The Lakers won 104–100.

Wilt puts one up and in against the New York Knicks during the 1972 playoff finals.

Now they were Western Conference champions.

For the league championship the Lakers had to meet the New York Knicks, the same team that had beaten them for the title in 1970. The Knicks won the opening game, 114–92, but then the Lakers swept the next four in a row. There was never a doubt which team was best, and Chamberlain was the best of them all.

Wilt blocked shot after shot. He scored 97 points in the five games and grabbed 116 rebounds. He even contributed 13 assists. He made 39 of 65 field-goal shots, for an average of almost 60 percent.

In the final game, Wilt's physical condition was a question mark. He had taken a bad fall in the fourth game and seriously sprained his right wrist. The Lakers didn't know whether he would be able to play at all. But he played. With his wrist heavily bandaged, Chamberlain scored 24 points and pulled down 29 rebounds. The Lakers won, 114–100. It was all over.

West cried again in the locker room, but this time with joy. He gave all the credit to his giant teammate: "Wilt? He was simply the guy that got us here. Without him we could not have even reached the final."

Wilt Chamberlain was nearly 36 years old then, an age when most players would be ready to retire. But Wilt was in such good shape that he seemed likely to continue playing for a long time. If anyone could do it, he could. In a land of giants, Wilt Chamberlain was truly a big man.

Kareem Abdul-Jabbar

After just two years in the NBA, Kareem Abdul-Jabbar was already being hailed as the best center in the history of pro basketball. But even more exciting was the prospect of the years to come, for he seemed bound to get much, much better.

Abdul-Jabbar, who was known as Lew Alcindor before legally taking the Islamic name in 1971, was a basketball star from the time he began playing in grammar school and in the parks and playgrounds of New York City. Even then, he was not only bigger than anyone else—he was better.

Naturally, a large part of his success was due to his great height. No one ever seemed to know exactly how tall Kareem really was, but one thing was certain—he was even taller than his team said he was. The Milwaukee Bucks claimed that Abdul-Jabbar was 7-foot-1, but the men who played against him knew he was taller, perhaps 7-foot-4.

His size was not the only thing that made Abdul-Jabbar great, though. He was a superb athlete, and while there were others nearly as tall, no one came even close to him in all-around ability. He combined his rare height with all the speed, quickness and coordination of a much smaller man. In fact, many scouts and coaches felt he would have made a fine NBA forward if he had been much shorter.

Abdul-Jabbar dominated a game as no one else ever had. His shots, especially his baseline hooks, were just about impossible to block. Few centers could rebound well against him, and none had as much potential on defense.

But despite his incredible talent, Abdul-Jabbar was not without problems. In fact, it was his unusual ability that was responsible for most of his difficulties.

"People think it's too easy for me to play well," he once said. "They think I don't even try hard. They resent me when I have an easy time and help to beat their team. But that's only part of it. People are never satisfied with me. If I have just an ordinary game, they think I'm loafing. I always have to be the best, do the most, score all the points and block all the shots.

"When I graduated high school I was expected to become an All-America player in college. When I joined the pros I was expected to become an All-Star right away. If I do these things, if I live up to the idea everyone has of me, then it's nothing special because they expected it all along."

His fans expected Kareem to be perfect off the court as well as on it. When he failed to live up to their image of a superstar, he was harshly criticized.

Some people said he was unfriendly and moody, that he kept to himself and was difficult to talk to. But those who knew him had some idea of the problems he had to live with. He was so much taller than anyone else that he couldn't go anywhere without being recognized. As a black man he experienced some forms of prejudice, and being the center of attention was not always pleasant.

Kareem was born on April 16, 1947, in New York City. His parents named him Ferdinand Lewis Alcindor, Jr., after his father. Until he was three years old he lived in Harlem, but then his family moved to the Dyckman Housing Project in upper Manhattan.

The Dyckman Project was 85 percent white, and nearly all of Kareem's friends were white.

"Dyckman was not a ghetto," he explained. "It was green, as green as California, and we never wanted for anything important."

But the prejudice was still very real. Kareem's father was a graduate of the famous Juilliard School of Music in New York City, but that never helped him earn a living. Although he was a talented musician, he worked first as a bill collector for a furniture company, then later as a police officer in the New York City subway system.

Kareem attended St. Jude's Catholic School through the third grade. But then both his parents went to work, and that left no one at home to care for him. So Kareem was sent to Holy Providence School in Cornwell, Pennsylvania.

At Holy Providence he met many black young-
sters from ghetto backgrounds. They came from
Philadelphia, Baltimore and Washington, D.C., and
Kareem had never known such children before.

"At St. Jude's there had been just one other
black," he remembered. "But my classmates at Holy
Providence were deprived black kids. These were
tough, hardened little fellows. I got off on the wrong
foot with them because I could read well and easily.
The nuns made a big deal about how well I read,
and that did it. They looked at me like I was some
kind of wierd egghead. But when basketball season
began, I noticed they did a lot of friendly looking in
my direction. I was already the second-tallest in the
school—and it went up to the eighth grade."

Kareem stayed at Holy Providence just one year.
By the fifth grade he was back in New York,
attending St. Jude's. It was then that he developed a
love for all sports. In addition to basketball he
played baseball and football and ran for the track
team.

When it was time to enter high school several of
the city's parochial schools tried to "recruit" Kareem
for his basketball talent. But his parents did not
want sports to be the only thing in their son's life.
"The first choice was education," said his father.
"We were determined to bring Lewis up properly
and to give him proper goals. We are proud of his
basketball talents, but we are just as proud of his
education and his college degree."

The Alcindors decided to send their son to Power
Memorial High School, a Catholic school run by the

Irish Christian Brothers in Manhattan. Power Memorial had a reputation for its excellent teachers and students, but its basketball team was hardly first rate. When Kareem decided that Power was for him, the coach and students were overjoyed.

Power's coach, Jack Donohue, soon became a very important person in the young athlete's life. "When I first saw him," said Donohue, "he was playing on the St. Jude's team. I thought I was dreaming. Lots of coaches dream about finding such a tall, coordinated player in grammar school. But other coaches wake up from those dreams. I already was awake, and there he was."

Strangely enough, Kareem's first game for Power was disappointing. Although he was only a freshman, he started at center for the varsity. But Power lost to LaSalle Academy, and Kareem was outplayed by Val Reid, who later became a star at Syracuse University.

"But Lew worked hard," Donohue recalled. "He never backed away from work. Even after our practices were finished he'd stay on the court to shoot. It was just a matter of time before he learned how to use all the ability he had. All it took was hard work."

The effort more than paid off, and by his sophomore season Kareem was already a star. "I was beginning to get the idea of how to use my size, and when other teams ganged up on me I learned how to pass off. So there was really no effective way to stop us, and nobody did."

That's right. Nobody did. Power won all 27 games

it played, and Kareem was named to every High School All-America team.

Basketball became a major part of his life, and he spent that summer at Donohue's basketball camp, Friendship Farm, in upstate New York. There he continued to polish his skills, and in his junior year he was better than ever. Power had another perfect season, 25–0, and again Kareem was All-America.

In Kareem's senior year it began to look as if Power's winning streak would never end. The team racked up one victory after another against some tough competition. One of its proudest triumphs was against DeMatha High of Washington, D.C., a team which included future Notre Dame stars Bob Whitmore and Sid Catlett as well as Bernie Williams, who went on to become an All-America at LaSalle College and a player in the NBA.

Kareem and Power Memorial extended their streak to 71 wins before they faced DeMatha again. That meeting was widely advertised, and to play it DeMatha got permission to use the nearby University of Maryland fieldhouse. A crowd of more than 15,000 watched as DeMatha upset Power, 46–43.

Kareem was crushed. "He cried in the locker room," Donohue recalled. "He told me it was all his fault, that if he had played better it wouldn't have happened. He had scored only sixteen points, and I told him it was because DeMatha slowed down the game to have a chance at winning."

Kareem (33) drops the ball in the hoop in a 1965 game between Power Memorial and Rice High School.

"I told him that we would never have won seventy-one in a row without him, that DeMatha was the second-best high school team in the country and that without him that night we might have lost by forty points. But it didn't help much. I never saw a kid who hated to lose as much as he did. Also, I honestly feel we had forgotten how to lose."

Kareem went on to finish out his senior year without another loss, which made his four-year varsity record 79–2. Power never lost a New York City League game, and the team won three consecutive city championships.

During Kareem's junior and senior years scouts and recruiters from every college in the country had found their way to Power Memorial. There were hundreds of them, and Donohue was afraid they would pressure his star. Kareem was the most wanted player in America's high schools, and Donohue knew it was a difficult situation for a 17-year-old boy to handle.

So the coach took over. He had Kareem's parents change their telephone number, and he told all the colleges to send their letters and their men to the high school. He told Kareem not to talk to any scouts or coaches or even members of the press.

But Kareem wasn't the only one being pursued. Because of the outstanding work he had done with his young star, many colleges wanted Donohue to become their coach. Most of them, however, only wanted Donohue if he would bring Kareem with him, and the coach wasn't interested in that kind of a deal. "Those offers made no sense to me,"

Donohue said. "I could see they didn't really want me, just Lew. I threw those letters away."

But Holy Cross University really wanted Donohue, and he accepted the job once he was sure there were no strings attached to the offer. When he accepted the position, however, many people assumed Kareem would go to Holy Cross, too. They couldn't believe Donohue was that honorable.

Donohue was certainly an honorable man—but it wasn't always easy. "As a college coach, I suddenly became one of those who wanted him to play for me," he admitted. "But I never asked him to do it. I mentioned it once, and he took a trip with me to Worcester just to see the school. But he never really wanted Holy Cross, and I never pushed him."

Finally, after listening to offers from more than 250 schools, Kareem narrowed his choice down to four—St. John's and New York University, both in New York City, and the University of Michigan and the University of California at Los Angeles (UCLA). "I guess it really was a choice of staying home or going away," he said. "I loved New York. All my friends were there and my parents were there. It would have been a lot of fun to play in the city."

But for several reasons, he finally decided against New York and in favor of UCLA. "I felt it would be good for me to travel, to see how people lived in another part of the country. I remember even as a kid I had always been curious about California. So I guess that made up my mind. I had traveled to see the campus and to meet with Coach John Wooden. It was beautiful out there, and I was impressed with

Towering over a crowd of newsmen, Kareem announces his decision to attend UCLA.

Wooden. He had never pressured me, and his attitude was that he would be happy to have me, but if I chose another place, fine. I liked that."

When Kareem had made his choice, Donohue suggested that he tell everybody at once, not just UCLA. "If he didn't make a public announcement, all those other people would keep pestering him," the coach said. "I suggested that he hold a press conference so everybody would know right away."

Kareem agreed, and on May 4, 1965, in the gymnasium of Power Memorial High, he and Donohue stood surrounded by television lights and cameras, radio microphones and more than 50 newspapermen.

After shifting nervously from one foot to the other, he finally spoke into the microphones. "This fall I'll be attending UCLA in Los Angeles," Kareem said. "That's the decision I came to. It has everything I want in a school."

So Kareem made the 3,000-mile journey from New York to California. When he played his first game as a freshman UCLA knew he was going to be one of the very special players in history.

The freshman team had several former high school stars. Even without Kareem, it would have developed into a super varsity team. With him, it became unbelievable. Among the other players were Lucius Allen and Kenny Heitz at the guard positions and Lynn Shackleford and Kent Taylor at forward. And of course there was Kareem Abdul-Jabbar (who was still known as Lew Alcindor) at center.

The previous season (1964–65) the UCLA varsity had won the national championship, and most of those players were back for their senior year. So it was not expected to be much of a game when the UCLA varsity played its annual game against the freshman team in November.

It certainly wasn't much of a game. The Bruin varsity never had a chance. Kareem's freshmen friends won the game, 75–60. Against the national varsity champions, Kareem scored 31 points, grabbed 15 rebounds and blocked shot after shot.

One Los Angeles newspaper account told the whole story in one sentence: "The varsity is the number one team in the country—and the number two team on its campus."

That was the high point of Kareem's freshman season, for no freshman team offered half the challenge of the UCLA varsity. The team finished with a 21–0 record, and Kareem averaged 33.1 points and 21.5 rebounds per game. For the rest of the season the freshmen averaged 113.2 points per game, limiting their opposition to an average of 56.6. In one game against Citrus Junior College, UCLA won by 103 points.

Nevertheless, Kareem was happy when the season ended because he was eager to join the varsity, where he could play against better teams. On December 3, 1966, he played his first varsity game against the University of Southern California, UCLA's crosstown rival.

Kareem scored 56 points, and UCLA won easily. The giant center leaped to seemingly impossible heights to grab a pass, and then stuffed the ball through the hoop on his way down. He made 23 of 32 field-goal attempts and ten of 14 free throws. Nobody could get near him to rebound, and nobody was able to block any of his shots.

Kareem was so good it was almost frightening.

Kareem begins his varsity career with a dunk shot against Southern California.

Coach Wooden, perhaps the finest college basketball coach in the country, said, "Lewis has no idea of what he can do. I know what he does to another team, and I feel sympathy for them. He is coachable and a team player. He will get much, much better. He is awesome."

Other teams quickly realized Kareem could not be stopped by ordinary means, so they tried to intimidate him. He was pushed and kicked and elbowed and tripped, but nothing stopped him. His rivals had wanted Kareem to lose his temper, but he didn't. He controlled his anger and played better than ever. "I was used to that from New York," he said. "I expected it to happen, and I've always been afraid of losing my cool. I just tried to do my best and hoped the referees would see the fouls and call them."

Some of the less honorable teams tried to anger him with insults, especially racial slurs. "I never even heard that jive," he said. "It hurt to know that people would do it, but I didn't let it affect my game."

The season continued and victory followed victory. The Bruins wound up with a 30–0 record, another national championship bid and an All-America center—Kareem Abdul-Jabbar.

At the NCAA championship in Louisville, Kentucky, UCLA met Houston in the semifinals. The match attracted national attention because Houston's star center was another All-America, Elvin Hayes. The 6-foot-9 Hayes was considered the only player in the country who had a chance to beat Kareem. Hayes did score 25 points to Kareem's 19, and he had 24 rebounds to Kareem's 20. But UCLA won, 73–58, in a game that was never close.

Despite UCLA's triumph, Hayes was outspoken in his criticism of Kareem. "He's not really all that good, you know," said the disappointed Hayes. "He's not especially strong and he can be moved out from under the boards. I think we can take care of him, and I think we can beat UCLA. Lew just isn't aggressive enough, and he stands around too much."

But Kareem and the Bruins must have been doing something right. UCLA went on to the final round and scored an easy 79–64 victory over Dayton for the NCAA championship.

Kareem's first varsity season had ended just the way everybody thought it would. UCLA and Kareem had gone undefeated. UCLA and Kareem had won the national championship. Kareem himself had become the first sophomore in many years to be a unanimous All-America choice. And both the major news agencies in the country—United Press International and Associated Press—named him the Player of the Year.

Things couldn't have gone better for Kareem, but there was one problem. He was homesick. "UCLA is just great," he said, "but it would be perfect if they could move the campus to New York City. I do miss my family and my friends."

As soon as his feelings became known, all the universities that had once tried to recruit him saw new hope. Rumors quickly spread that the super-center was going to transfer to a college closer to home, maybe St. John's, maybe NYU. One report

even claimed he was going to leave UCLA to enroll at Princeton.

But Kareem laughed at all the rumors. "I may be homesick," he said, "but I love the school and the team and the kids out here. I'll just have to get used to being homesick. I can always come home during the summers, and that will have to be enough for me."

Once he said that, the question never came up again. But as soon as Kareem returned to UCLA for his junior year he had to deal with another problem.

The coaches of UCLA's rivals knew that Kareem was better than any of their best stars and pressured the Rules Committee of the NCAA to "try to do something to stop him." Their complaints were too loud for the NCAA to ignore, and so the "Alcindor Rule" was established. It outlawed Kareem's favorite "dunk" shot, the stuff-the-ball-through-the-basket shot the fans loved to see.

But even that couldn't stop him. Kareem simply jumped and dropped the ball through the hoop. And, of course, nothing could stop him from rebounding and playing his octopus defense.

In 1967–68, UCLA won its first 17 games and then came face-to-face with Houston, which was ranked second in the country that season. It was a long-awaited meeting, especially for Elvin Hayes. The game was played on January 20, 1968, before a crowd of 52,693 in the Houston Astrodome. More

Arch-rivals Abdul-Jabbar and Elvin Hayes of Houston fight for the ball in the 1967 NCAA semi-finals.

than 150 television stations would carry it around the country.

But the week before the big game, UCLA played the University of California, and Kareem's eyeball was scratched in a scramble under the boards. The big center was bothered with double vision and headaches. In order to clear it up, coach Wooden kept him out of the next two games, and told him to stay in bed. "It worked a little, but it made me terribly out of shape," Kareem recalled. "When we played Houston, I was exhausted when the game wasn't more than five minutes old. I still had vision problems, too.

"With all this going for Houston, how many points did they beat us by? Two! Just two. We felt we were surely still number one. But the polls didn't believe it. I was the worst player on the court, but the coach let me stay in and blow the game. I thanked him for his confidence, but that night he would have been better off taking me out."

UCLA's winning streak was over. Houston had beaten them 71–69, and Hayes had been the star. He scored 39 points to Kareem's 15 and had 15 rebounds to Kareem's 12.

After that Hayes was more boastful than ever. Kareem was bitterly disappointed, but all he had to say was, "I wish Houston luck, because I don't want to see any other team beat them until we get our chance."

The teams would meet again, in March, if they kept winning and earned another NCAA Tournament invitation. And that's just what they did. The date was March 22, 1968. The place was the Los Angeles Sports Arena. Again, it was the semifinal game of the tournament.

Kareem had spent the last months of the season with a cover from *Sports Illustrated* pasted in his locker, showing Hayes scoring over him. "I wanted to remember," he said.

Never before had any team played as well in such an important game and against such a talented opponent. Houston didn't stand a chance. With the score 20–19 in favor of UCLA, the Bruins went on a spurt and made it 37–24. UCLA had a 22-point lead at halftime, and when it reached a margin of 44 points in the second half, all the substitutes were sent in to mop up.

Kareem walked off the court with 2:04 still to play, his right arm upraised with the index finger telling the world that his team—and he, too—was still Number One! The final score: UCLA 101, Houston 69.

The next night UCLA easily beat North Carolina, 78–55, for another NCAA championship. North Carolina coach Dean Smith said that "this is the best team of all time and Alcindor is the greatest who ever played college basketball."

With the season over, Kareem had a tough decision to make. He had been invited to Mexico City as a member of the U.S. Olympic basketball team, but some professional players who lived in Harlem wanted him to spend his summer there and work with the ghetto kids.

Kareem went to Harlem. The program, called

Operation Sports Rescue, was sponsored by New York City, and Kareem felt it was worthwhile. "We worked in Harlem and in Bedford-Stuyvesant and in Brownsville," he said, speaking of other ghetto areas in the city. "I was talking to little black kids who are going to suffer because they don't have any examples they can model themselves on. They dig ball, so they dig me. If I can change ten who would become junkies and make them useful citizens, that's the most important thing I can do right now."

Kareem had decided not to compete in the Olympics because he felt, "it's wrong to represent this nation and then have to come home and face the music of prejudice all over again."

It was in that summer of 1968 that the man known as Lew Alcindor began to call himself Kareem Abdul-Jabbar, after reading the words of Malcolm X. He joined an Islamic sect, whose philosophy is to "try for change as quickly and as painlessly as possible. Try to stand for something positive, like people, young people, trying to help each other."

After that summer Kareem returned to UCLA for his senior year and found that nothing had changed. There was still no team capable of beating the Bruins, and winning every game was getting almost boring. Even coach Wooden was becoming restless. After UCLA won the Holiday Festival, a Christmas-time tournament in New York's Madison Square Garden, he spoke of Kareem's upcoming graduation. "I'll be glad to go back to coaching to win again, instead of coaching not to lose," he said.

Not surprisingly, Kareem's college career ended with a third straight NCAA championship. The Bruins had a brief scare in the semifinal against Drake, but finally won, 85–82. After that the championship game was a breeze. UCLA beat a good Purdue team, with All-America scoring star Rick Mount, 92–72. In that final game Kareem scored 37 points and took down 20 rebounds. For the third straight year he was chosen as the tournament's Most Valuable Player.

Kareem finished his three varsity seasons at UCLA (a total of 88 games) with a 26.4-point scoring average and the record for field-goal accuracy. He made 943 of 1,476 shots for a hard-to-believe 63.9 percentage. It had been a sensational chapter in his life, but Kareem was ready for something new.

"I was relieved when the college part of my career ended," he said. "I didn't enjoy the pressure of having to win every game. I wish people would have left me alone. There were times I really resented it."

Coach Wooden understood his star player's feelings. "Lewis couldn't help the situation," he said, "because it was his great talent that created it. I think he'll do just fine as a professional. And I don't think he has yet reached his peak."

There was no doubt about it—Kareem was ready for pro ball. That had been his goal ever since he had first played basketball in grammar school. "I'd go to the Garden to see the Knicks," he recalled, "and I got to meet many of the visiting stars. I enjoyed that. Now I was going to play against them."

The basketball net draped over his neck, Kareem flashes three fingers to indicate UCLA's third straight championship.

Kareem wasn't the only one looking forward to his debut as a professional. There wasn't a single team in the ABA or NBA that didn't want the college superstar on their side. When the 1968 draft came up, it was obvious that Kareem Abdul-Jabbar would be everyone's first choice.

In the NBA the Phoenix Suns and the Milwaukee Bucks, two new expansion teams, had tied with the worst records. So a coin flip was necessary to see which one would have the first draft pick.

In the ABA, the New York Nets were given the first chance to draft Kareem. Of course, all the other ABA teams wanted him, too. But they knew their league had to have him, and rather than lose him to the NBA, they agreed to give New York the chance. They knew Abdul-Jabbar was a New Yorker, and they thought he would be most likely to choose a team in his hometown.

Kareem knew how badly both leagues wanted him, and he didn't want to become the object of long, drawn-out bidding. So he and his advisers came up with a plan to avoid it. He would accept one offer from each league, then simply pick the highest.

In the NBA, the Bucks won the flip of the coin and so they had that league's first rights to Kareem. It became a guessing game—which team would offer more money, the Bucks or the Nets?

It turned out to be the Bucks. They offered a contract worth $1,400,000, while the Nets' offer was for $1,000,000. When Kareem said he would sign with Milwaukee, the other owners in the ABA became angry with Nets' owner Arthur Brown. They called Kareem's advisers and said the whole league would make an offer, with each team chipping in for a total of $3,250,000. It was much more money than the Bucks had offered, but Kareem turned it down. He had given his word.

"If I had to choose, and if the money was not important, I would have picked the Nets because of New York," Kareem said. "But a deal is a deal. I wouldn't listen to any late offers."

The ABA owners continued to make offers, but Kareem had made up his mind. He had given his word, and that was important to him.

The ABA was desperate because it was losing money. What it needed was a famous star, someone like Abdul-Jabbar. Another important consideration was the influence Kareem would have on other outstanding college players. "Most players like to play where the competition is the best," said one ABA owner. "If we had been able to sign Abdul-Jabbar, more and more top players would have chosen our league. Most of them would have been the great centers because that's where the challenge would have been, to see if they were better than him."

Kareem was excited at the thought of playing professionally. As a pro he could legally dunk the ball again. The NBA's 24-second clock would prevent teams from slowing down the game. Kareem would finally be able to play his own game.

Kareem's first NBA game was played on October 18, 1969, against the Detroit Pistons. It was shown on national television and, of course, there was a capacity crowd in the Milwaukee Arena. He scored 29 points, took down twelve rebounds, picked up six assists, made three steals and blocked 13 shots. The Bucks won, 119–110. It was a fine beginning. But Kareem wasn't satisfied. "I didn't care too much for the way I played," he said. "I made a lot of mistakes and I took some bad shots."

As the season progressed, however, Abdul-Jabbar made fewer mistakes and more and more good shots. Kareem—and basketball fans all over the country— looked forward to the day when he would meet another super-scoring center—Wilt Chamberlain of the Los Angeles Lakers.

Kareem was disappointed with his first showing against Chamberlain. Although both big men put on a dazzling display, Wilt scored 25 points to Kareem's 23 and grabbed 25 rebounds to his 20. "I learned a few things that night," Kareem admitted. "I was just a skinny kid out there, and he was the master."

That was the only meeting of the giants that season, because a knee injury kept Wilt out of action for the rest of the year.

As the long NBA season continued, however, Kareem improved almost every day. "I was worried at first that I wouldn't be strong enough to last through that long a season," he said. "But I used weights and I tried to build up my strength. I didn't want to get too heavy, because I wouldn't have my quickness. But Bill Russell never weighed a lot. He was skinny and he made it through all those years. I decided that if he could do it, so could I."

Milwaukee's coach, Larry Costello, had no doubts

about his young center's abilities, and he knew just how important Abdul-Jabbar was to the Bucks. "When we saw what a talent he had, we would have been foolish to use anything else but a center-offense," said Costello. "We tried to get the ball to him every chance we had. Some people criticize that, but to me it makes sense. Didn't the Cleveland Browns give the football to Jimmy Brown whenever they could? I owe it to the fans and to the team. If I don't get as much out of him as I can, I wouldn't be doing my job. He can win for us."

And win he did. "Nobody of his age has the same talents," said another big center, Willis Reed of the New York Knicks. "He's going to be the best center in the league."

Other players and coaches had the same words. "He is of superstar talent right now, and he has played only fifteen games," said Tom Heinsohn, coach of the Boston Celtics. "He combines the best talents of Russell and Chamberlain. He is a new force in professional basketball."

Abdul-Jabbar finished his rookie season with a 28.8-point-per-game average, second only to Laker Jerry West's league-leading 31.2. In addition, Kareem was third in rebounding and second in minutes played.

In 1968–69 the Bucks had been a ragged team, winning just 27 of their 82 games. But with Kareem they won 56 games in '69–70 to finish second in the

One-on-one, Abdul-Jabbar meets another big man—Wilt Chamberlain of the Los Angeles Lakers.

Eastern Division, just four games behind the New York Knicks.

Milwaukee's first playoff contest was against the Philadelphia 76ers. The Bucks won the best-of-seven series in five quick games.

Milwaukee's next opponent was New York, and that was a different story. No team in the league had ever played better team basketball than New York. No one Knick was counted on to win the game. All five were.

Such teams are difficult to beat, because stopping one player does not guarantee a victory. In the first game Kareem had 35 points and 15 rebounds, but the Knicks won, 110–102. In the second game he scored 38 points and had 23 rebounds, and again the Knicks won, 112–111. In that game, New York was ahead, 110–109, with 52 seconds to play. It was at that moment that Kareem missed two free throws.

In the third game Abdul-Jabbar showed everyone just what he could do. The Bucks won that game, 101–96, and Kareem enjoyed one of his best games ever. He scored 33 points, took down 31 rebounds and blocked eleven shots. "It is frightening what he can do," said the Knicks' Bill Bradley.

But that was the only game the Bucks were to win. The Knicks took the last two and gained the NBA finals against Los Angeles. (The Knicks won that series to become league champions for the first time in their 25-year history.)

Reed, still remembering what Kareem had done against him, was quick to praise the rookie giant. "When he learns to save motion and effort and just turn to the basket and shoot, I doubt if anyone in this league will be able to play with him, or even stay with him. In his first season he just wasn't sure of what was expected of him . . . but each time we played them he was better. The rest of us are just centers. He's a whole team."

New York coach Red Holzman tipped off the Knicks' secret to playing the Bucks and winning. "You have to be ready to give Abdul-Jabbar his forty points and twenty-five rebounds and concentrate on stopping everyone else. But it's getting harder to hold him to even those numbers."

The Bucks had made great progress since their super-center had joined them, but one man—even one like Kareem—couldn't do it all. What Milwaukee needed was an experienced guard, a veteran ball-handler who could pass to Kareem but who could score, too. The Bucks knew just the man for the job, but they weren't sure they could get him. His name was Oscar Robertson.

On May 3, 1970, Milwaukee announced the sensational news—they had traded guard Flynn Robinson and forward Charlie Paulk to Cincinnati for the Big O, the most famous guard in NBA history.

Now they were sure. Now they were ready.

Adding a man of Oscar's remarkable skills would not only make the Bucks a better team, it would make Kareem an even better player. The Bucks also

Back to back, Kareem and New York center Willis Reed fight for possession of the ball. ▶

traded to get Lucius Allen, Kareem's teammate, roommate and best friend from UCLA.

After the Robertson trade a *Sports Illustrated* reporter predicted: "Alcindor's improvement is going to amaze those who thought last season he could hardly be better. Oscar's presence as a playmaker and scorer will strengthen the team . . . a dynasty is in the making here."

The relationship between Kareem and Oscar blossomed instantly. During the summer, they both played in the Maurice Stokes Memorial Game in New York's Catskill Mountains. "We were on the same team," Kareem recalled. "He had the ball and he drove for the basket, and I cut the wrong way. Man, he yelled at me. When Oscar talks, you listen. He said 'Listen, you got to do it this way, my way.' I listened. The next time he drove, I cut the right way and he got the ball to me and I scored. I saw what he meant to me. Oscar wants that championship, right now. This year. And he's got us all feeling that way."

The 1970–71 season belonged to the Milwaukee Bucks, right from the opening game. They went on to win 66 of their 82 games, as Kareem led the league in scoring with a 31.7 per-game average and finished fourth in rebounding with 16 per game.

Robertson's value was obvious. He averaged 19.4 points per game and was third in the NBA in assists with 8.2 per game. Many of those assists wound up in Abdul-Jabbar's scoring column.

Detroit's Bob Lanier comes down hard on Kareem's shoulders, but the Buck center draws a blocking foul on the play.

"I never saw two players work that well together," coach Costello said. "It was like they knew
what the other one was going to do almost before
they did it. Oscar helped Kareem, and because of
the big man in the middle Oscar became an even
better player than he already was. It was just
beautiful to watch."

The playoffs that year were everything the Bucks
could have wished. In the first round Milwaukee
beat San Francisco in five games, holding the
Warriors to fewer than 100 points in three of the
games and winning the final one by an incredible
score of 136–86.

Next Milwaukee met Los Angeles for the Western
Conference championship, another one-sided series.
Again the Bucks won the series in five games.

The Bucks' only disappointment came in the
finals, but it was a minor one. The team they had
hoped to meet for the NBA championship was the
Knicks, but New York, after waltzing past Atlanta in
five games, had been upset by the Baltimore Bullets
in a tight, seven-game series.

"We really did want to play the Knicks again,
because we were sure we could have beaten them.
But playing for the championship is an honor, no
matter who you have to play." That was Kareem's
feeling, and he spoke for the rest of the Bucks.

So the Bucks played the Bullets for the title, and it
was never even close. Milwaukee took the cham-

*Kareem drives past Chamberlain to score an uncontested goal in
the 1971 playoffs.*

pionship in four straight games. In three of the
games the Bullets failed to reach 100 points.

Abdul-Jabbar had the finest series of any player in
the history of the league. The tallest center in the
NBA, Kareem was matched against one of the
smallest, Baltimore's 6-foot-8 Wes Unseld. In the
first game, Kareem had 31 points and 17 rebounds.
In the second, he had 27 points and 24 rebounds. In
the third, he scored 23 points with 22 rebounds, and
in the final game, he scored 27 points with a dozen
rebounds. Naturally, he was voted the Most Valuable Player in the playoffs.

By Kareem's third professional season (1971–72)
he was already recognized as the top center in the
game. His statistics supported that claim, as he led
the league in scoring with a 34.8 average, and
finished third with 16.6 rebounds per game. His
370 assists gave him the second highest total on his
team.

Nevertheless, the Bucks ran into a bit of trouble
when they reached the playoffs after a 63–19 season.
They had to play the outstanding Lakers again, a
team that had set records by the book-full during the
season.

One of the records was an unbelievable 33 game
winning streak, the longest by any team in any
professional sport. It was finally ended by—who
else?—the Bucks. The score was 120–104, and a
nationwide television audience watched the great
match-up of Abdul-Jabbar and Chamberlain. Wilt
was in control until the third quarter, when he
picked up his fourth personal foul. But he had to be

careful after that, and Kareem was able to score several important baskets. Then the big Buck set up a screen for Lucius Allen, and Allen's basket put the Bucks ahead for good.

With Milwaukee and Los Angeles scheduled to meet in the semi-finals most people expected the Bucks to win even though the Lakers had had such an excellent season.

In the first game, it looked as if they were right. Milwaukee's defense was sensational. The Lakers connected on just 27 percent of their shots, and the Bucks won, 93–72. In that game LA's Jim McMillian made three of 20 shots, Jerry West four of 19, and Gail Goodrich two of 14. But the Lakers squeaked through to win the second game, 135–134.

The third game ended in a three-point Los Angeles victory, and it was the old Chamberlain magic on defense that kept the Lakers on top. He held Abdul-Jabbar scoreless during a nearly twelve-minute stretch, blocking five of his shots. With the Lakers out in front, Kareem broke loose and scored four baskets in a row to tie up the game. It stayed close until the fourth quarter, when Wilt held Kareem without a field goal for the final eleven minutes.

Milwaukee ran away with the fourth game, 114–88, but the Lakers won the fifth, 115–90. In the sixth game Milwaukee held a ten-point lead in the fourth quarter. But then Wilt took over, blocking shots and grabbing all the rebounds. In the final eight minutes, the Lakers outscored the Bucks by twelve points. That was enough to deny Kareem Abdul-Jabbar a second straight championship. Los Angeles won the game, 104–100, and the series, four games to two.

Most of the Lakers felt they had just won the championship, even though they still had to play the Knicks in the finals. "Wilt was the guy who got us here," said Jerry West. "The way he played Abdul-Jabbar was the difference."

"In all the years I've seen professional basketball," said Bob Cousy, who after a great career with the Boston Celtics became head coach of the Kansas City–Omaha Kings, "I don't think I've seen a center like Abdul-Jabbar. He has the qualities of Chamberlain and Russell, who were the two best. He uses the great mental concentration of Russell with the overpowering strength and ability of Chamberlain. It's really impossible to stop him. There's not a lot you can do."

Abdul-Jabbar was all alone at the top of the basketball world. Russell had retired and Chamberlain was nearing that age. There were no young centers whose abilities even approached his. Bob Lanier of the Detroit Pistons, Elmore Smith of the Buffalo Braves, Dave Cowens of the Boston Celtics and Neal Walk of the Phoenix Suns were good young centers, but none of them matched Kareem. Such superb veterans as Walt Bellamy of the Atlanta Hawks and Nate Thurmond of the Golden State Warriors sometimes played even with Kareem, but neither of them was able to do that more than a few times each season.

Some NBA coaches considered Kareem a one-man team. "If you take him away, Milwaukee is no better than Portland," said Chicago coach Dick Motta during the winter of 1973. (Portland was then one of the league's weakest teams.) "Their other four starters can be handled, but not him."

It was a reasonable statement. At the time, the other four starters for the Bucks were Oscar Robertson and Lucius Allen at guard, Bob Dandridge and Curtis Perry at forward. Although they were outstanding players, so was almost every starter on every other team. But still, there was no one like Kareem Abdul-Jabbar.

"Even more than Wilt or Russell, this man can change an entire team," Motta continued. "If I was starting a brand new team and if I had my choice of any player in the country, I'd take Abdul-Jabbar."

After just three years as a pro Kareem was almost a legend. He played nearly every minute of every game. He continued to improve. He worked hard to perfect his hook shot, and he tried to learn better ways of getting position for rebounds.

"It's his defense," says Russell, the man who should know. "He has learned to use timing and that's much better than just jumping as high as you can. He's not watching the shooter any more, he's watching the ball. I think he will be remembered as the greatest center ever."

Index

Pages numbers in italics refer to photographs.